Until the Trumpet Sounds

until the trumpet sounds
SEEKING HOLINESS NOW

Zachary Grant, O.F.M. Cap.

ST. ANTHONY MESSENGER PRESS
Cincinnati, Ohio

Scripture citations are taken from the *New Revised Standard Version Bible*, copyright ©1989 by the Division of Christian Education of the National Council of Churches of Christ in the United States of America, and used by permission. All rights reserved.

Cover and book design by Mark Sullivan

Library of Congress Cataloging-in-Publication Data
Grant, Zachary.
  Until the trumpet sounds : seeking holiness now / Zachary Grant.
      p. cm.
   ISBN 0-86716-629-0 (alk. paper)
   1. Christian life—Catholic authors. 2. Holiness—Catholic Church. I.
Title.
   BX2350.3.G725 2005
   234'.8—dc22

                              2004024677

ISBN 0-86716-629-0
Copyright ©2005, Zachary Grant

Published by St. Anthony Messenger Press
www.AmericanCatholic.org
Printed in the U.S.A.

05 06 07 08 09 10 5 4 3 2 1

We will not all die,
but we will all be changed, in a moment,
in the twinkling of an eye,
at the last trumpet.
For the trumpet will sound,
And the dead will be raised imperishable,
and we will be changed.
1 Corinthians 15:51–52

acknowledgments

A special word of thanks and deep appreciation must go to my Capuchin brother Seán Patrick O'Malley, archbishop of Boston, who, in spite of the numerous responsibilities that devour his time, graciously accepted my fraternal request to write the Foreword for this book.

I also humbly recognize the one person who prodded my procrastinating nature until this book became a reality. Ms. Sandra Spazioso had read the reflections that I had written for the weekly bulletin of St. Francis Chapel in Springfield, Massachusetts, and she often urged me to put them in book form.

Her encouragement and prayers over the years strengthened my determination to bring this work to completion. She also reviewed the manuscript, and her suggestions to clarify certain points were gladly incorporated into the final text.

My sister, Lettie Cole, her son, Matt Jr., and a friend of long-standing, Mrs. John Leavitt, assured me of a positive response from the many lay Catholics who are seeking support in the pursuit of holiness. Two Sisters of St. Joseph from Holyoke, Massachusetts, contributed their special professional skills in reviewing the manuscript. Sister Patricia Smith is an experienced retreat director and spiritual counselor, and Sister Mary Anne Nolan is a proofreader and production associate for the *Catholic Observer,* the newspaper for the Diocese of Springfield.

May the God who first loved us bless all who generously shared their gifts for the glory of his name!

contents

Foreword *xv*
by Archbishop Seán Patrick O'Malley

Prologue *xix*

Chapter One: Seeking Holiness *1*
The eternal plan for each of us *3*
Sainthood is a noble ambition. *5*
To blossom where we are planted *7*
One size gospel fits all. *9*
Jesus our constant companion *13*
Only a modified pessimism makes sense. *16*
We are bound hand and foot. *18*
Ready to proceed *21*

Chapter Two: The Ground Rules *25*
Rule 1: *Listen up!* *26*
Rule 2: *Be honest with yourself.* *28*
Rule 3 *Forget about feeling holy.* *32*
Rule 4: *Forgive ahead of time.* *34*
Rule 5: *Look Jesus in the eye.* *35*
Rule 6: *Simplify your life.* *37*
Rule 7: *Expect love and tears to mix.* *40*
Rule 8: *Calm down!* *42*
Rule 9: *Learn from your troubles.* *45*
Rule 10: *Stand tall!* *48*

Chapter Three: The Breath of the Spirit *51*
Prayer is a two-way street. *52*
We believe Jesus, who is Truth. *55*
Our Father, who art in heaven... *57*

Hallowed be thy name. 60
Thy kingdom come. 62
Thy will be done on earth as it is in heaven. 63
Never trust a stranger! 65
Give us this day our daily bread. 66
Forgive us our trespasses as we forgive... 68
And lead us not into temptation, but... 71
Loving God is not a gamble. 72

Chapter Four: A Divine Conspiracy 75
Mothers know best. 77
Mary's first love 79
You can't be serious! 81
With Jesus and Mary 83
"Here is your Mother" (John 19:27). 85
Mothers are always mothers. 87
Why don't we do it "my way"? 90
Alert for warning signs 91
Source of our joy 94
The measure of holiness 96

Chapter Five: Betrayal 99
More than a voice in our ear 100
Sin is just under the surface. 103
Confession is no laughing matter. 105
No ground between sin and virtue 106
Being sorry is not enough. 109
The many faces of sin 111
Begone, Satan! 114
God is not finished with you yet! 116

Chapter Six: The Game Plan of Virtues *119*
Can the blind have a favorite color? 120
Living on promises 122
Don't look down! 124
There are no lazy saints. 125
Staying connected 127
Foolishness comes in two sizes. 129
I thirst for gratitude. 131
Courtesy begets goodness. 133
Ever been bored to tears? 135
The signs of success 137

Chapter Seven: Dying with Christ *141*
A new set of values 142
Mary carried a cross, too. 144
We are always self-centered. 146
Jesus suffers with us. 149
Pain is a source of wisdom. 151
The temptation of saints 154
Carry your own cross! 156
The Mass reflects our oneness. 158
Son and mother together again 161

Chapter Eight: Better Days Ahead *163*
Spiritual relationships are eternal. 165
Eyes on the horizon 167
To forget is possible. 171
Saints are never lonely. 174
The deficiencies of human judgment 178
The continuing guidance of Mary 180
Home is where the heart is. 183

foreword

The metaphor that describes our natural life from birth to death as a journey also expresses our growth in the life of grace. Love is not a static existence, but is a steady advance toward a union with God that, when the trumpet sounds, will find us in the eternal embrace of the Lord.

As with all adventures, the spiritual journey has moments of wonder and excitement that encourage us, and there are times of painful difficulties that might tempt us to turn back. *Until the Trumpet Sounds* reviews this spiritual journey toward holiness. The reflections that are offered can help us toward the fullness of God's love that awaits our generous response. Impelled by the grace of the Holy Spirit, we seek to respond to the call for holiness with all the energy that we are capable of.

Until the Trumpet Sounds considers the journey of the soul as a steady advance toward holiness. Each pair of chapters covers the necessary and complementary aspects of a healthy spirituality.

One and Two: The meaning and the parameters
                 of holiness
Three and Four: Our prayer life and our relation-
                 ship with Jesus and Mary
Five and Six: Sin and virtue
Seven and Eight: Death and resurrection

Father Zachary focuses on our individual journey in seeking intimacy with Jesus. However, he never separates Jesus from his church as the instrument and sacrament of salvation, or indeed from Mary as the mother of the church. Holiness is considered not only the purpose of the church's mission but also as a challenge to all the baptized that they participate in the new evangelization. Holiness is indispensable for the renewal and healing of the church in our day, as it has been in every age.

The church is holy because she possesses the means to bring each of us to union with the Triune God. As the Body of Christ brought together in a unity of faith through baptism, the church is Christ's presence in the world and gives praise to the Father by the power of the Holy Spirit. In each era of the church's history, men and women of heroic sanctity have been raised up to bring new life to the church. Pope John Paul II, in bringing to "the honors of the altar" so many new saints and blessed, provides us many examples of holiness for the present day. The challenge to all of us who serve the church is to be holy, because holiness is the only truly effective force for true evangelization and renewal. Trust in the gospel must underline bold changes. New programs that might alleviate social injustices can reduce the church to an organized charity if they fail to address the individual dignity of all God's children, especially the "least of my brothers." Only holy theologians, holy bishops, holy priests and holy laity can produce true renewal of spirit in the church.

The virtue of humility is the foundation of holiness. We might all take to heart the observation of Blessed Teresa of Calcutta when she insisted that Jesus does not expect us to be successful, only faithful. As a brother of Saint Francis, I am motivated in my apostolic service as priest and bishop by the words of Christ from the cross to the young man of Assisi who knelt in the chapel of San Damiano: *Repair my church!* Francis determined to imitate the way of Jesus in service to God's people. This, too, is my path to holiness. May *Until the Trumpet Sounds* be helpful to us all on our journey.

Archbishop Seán Patrick O'Malley, O.F.M. Cap.

prologue

In reviewing the lives of the saints, our examples of heroic Christian lives, we note that some journeys toward holiness were short. Anthony of Padua (or Lisbon) died at thirty-five years of age. Thérèse of Lisieux reached the age of only twenty-four. Maria Goretti had just attained her adolescence and was already worthy of a martyr's death. From the perspective of my senior years, these facts have sometimes made me uncomfortable. Has my lack of resolve in seeking holiness tested the patience of God? Will he give me enough time to catch up? I can, fortunately, take comfort in the knowledge that some saints took even longer than the life span that was normal in their particular era. In the fifth century the great Augustine of Hippo took a bumpy seventy-six years.

The grace of the Holy Spirit, the source of all holiness, is measured out by the generosity that we demonstrate when we finally get serious about sanctity. Some saints gave all at an early age. For others, their resolve did not become evident until later. Saint Teresa of Avila lived a mediocre religious life until she was over forty. By that age others saints had already died, as we have indicated. At some point, however, all saints decide that they want to come close to Jesus their redeemer. When reviewing our own situation, we all need to ask: "Am I still holding back?"

I first thought that I might subtitle this book *A Handbook For Would-Be Saints* because it is directed to those who are serious about their relationship to God, about becoming holy. Those who truly desire union with the Triune God, who is Father, Son and Holy Spirit, will understand that holiness is the total surrender to God's will. But it does take a plan, since sanctity does not just happen.

A friend suggested that I call this book *Sainthood for Dummies,* because there are those who think that becoming a saint is a complicated business. I was tempted, because we are going to talk about something that is as simple as falling in love. Yet our experience also confirms that, although more complicated, to *fall out of love* is also very easy. To *grow* steadily and deeply in love, however, is a lifelong difficult task. The title suggested was indeed intriguing and attention-getting, but I did not want anyone to interpret it as *Sainthood Made Easy,* which is definitely not the case. There are no shortcuts and taking up one's cross is basic. Besides, the wisdom that enables us to respond to God's love comes as a gift directly from the Holy Spirit. So we have the title that attracted you to this book.

A simplistic approach that may have been necessary as a beginning when we were children (Jesus and I) may carry us to the threshold. Our vision, however, must eventually seek the horizon where Eternal Beauty dwells. A desire to reach that place must become a passion, challenged by the twists and turns that the journey will take. Whether for many years or a few months, we have already been traveling along the road to holiness. Perhaps the time has come to see how far we have advanced and how far we might still have to go on our journey.

In our day the church has made it clear that all of us (lay faithful, religious, priests and bishops) have been called to holiness of life. Our destiny is to be saints. Chapter five, number forty, of the Constitution of the Second Vatican Council *Lumen Gentium* reads: "It is therefore quite clear that all Christians in any state or walk of life are called to the fullness of Christian life and to the perfection of love." We cannot doubt that as creatures of intelligence and will, baptized and infused with divine life, holiness is within the reach of us all.

Everyone has been tempted at one time or another to be satisfied with mediocrity, with just "getting into heaven." We of mature years might wonder, at times, why we have not yet gone to our eternal reward, as have so many of our contemporaries. Is it only because we have still not reached the level of holiness to which God has destined us? We may feel it is even now too late for us to reach the heights. Still we know that God can work miracles of grace and conversion in whatever amount of time that might still be necessary. If so, we can be grateful for the divine patience.

For those who want to try again, or to pick up the pace, I offer the following pages of my own reflections and experiences that keep me steadfast, however stumbling, on my own path to holiness. I have used them in my guidance of other would-be saints who were unsure of the direction that the Spirit was leading them because several pathways had opened up. Many assured me that, after prayerful reflection, they were able to overcome the spiritual confusion that had caused uncertainty in their soul's encounter with God. My assistance was especially helpful when a feeling of guilt was part of their memories.

Certainly, none of us are newly born. The spiritual and physical elements of our nature carry with them a past that consists of successes and failures. We might benefit from an occasional visit to these former experiences for an assurance about present decisions, or to recall the effects of some prior faulty judgment. However, since life circumstances are always changing and our own interior life will have improved, prudence demands that we give little attention to our former successes or miseries.

Rather, attention must be given to our simultaneous climb up the mount of Tabor and the hill of Calvary. Both lead us heavenward. We press forward in alternating rhythms between Transfiguration and Crucifixion. To stop before we reach the top of either one is to slip backward.

Let our future begin today.

Zachary Grant, O.F.M. Cap.

CHAPTER ONE

seeking holiness

As God's chosen ones, holy and beloved,
clothe yourselves with compassion, kindness,
humility, meekness and patience.
—Colossians 3:12

To make sure of the goal and what it takes to point us in the right direction, we will first focus on the proper attitude required to live a holy life. A would-be saint must first determine to live a morally good life. Then there is need to understand exactly what it means to love God, since every rule for pursuing sanctity flows from the fundamental truth that God is love.

A man once complained to me that he was jealous of God. "And why?" I asked. "Because," he said, "my wife loves God more than she loves me." My response to the gentleman was direct: "Your envy is misplaced. She could not possibly love such a fine man as you if she had not loved God first." I explained that his wife did not differentiate between God and him or, for that matter, all her children. The closer she was to God, that is to Jesus and to his Father, in the bond of the Holy Spirit, the closer she was to her husband and her family, because God is *one* and so there is only *one* love. As children of God we all share in that one love, unless we deliberately abandon the source of our life and salvation through grievous sin.

The man's reaction to his wife's piety was indeed human and understandable. Some of us tend to think that divine love is a distinct category, that human love is separate from God's love. Those who seek to grow within this love of the Triune God soon learn that such love becomes more mysterious and expansive as their interior life of prayer intensifies. The finite mind of the human being finds it extremely difficult, if not downright impossible, to comprehend how God can love as individuals all his people from every time and age. Our human love tends to be focused on self and helps create the dilemma. We always find ourselves struggling with the desire to be exclusive in our relationships.

Selfishness is the enemy of love, whether we speak of our love for God or for a human person. As sinners, we struggle in being faithful to a life in union with God's will. Our failure reveals itself in the self-centered acts that distance us from our neighbor. Thus, holiness is impossible to achieve unless we have first become convinced that we have been called to it because of our baptism. Were we not baptized in the name of the Father and of the Son and of the Holy Spirit? Are we not, therefore, children of the God of love? And does not God want all his children to love him totally as he would love them if they would just allow him to?

The eternal plan for each of us

With the evidence we have in the Scriptures, from the prophets, that there has been and continues to be a divine plan for God's people, we can presume that we all fit in somewhere. We do not have as prominent a place as Abraham and Moses, as Samuel and Elias, or indeed as Mary and Joseph. Yet, knowing that the Father willed that the Son would become man, can we imagine that any of us were left out of that will? Rather, should we not consider that each of us has a supporting role as one of those redeemed by the death of Jesus on the cross? Did we not become his children at baptism and therefore entitled to his love?

As the years go on, I find myself watching young children who have just begun school and wondering what God has in mind for them in their future years. I know that by the time they have matured I will most likely have passed into eternal life. This sense became much stronger after a unique experience I had not many years ago. One Saturday afternoon, after having just baptized five little ones, I gathered the parents and godparents in the sanctuary for the final blessings from the ritual. I suggested that the children be placed on the altar itself as a sign that all the sacraments flow from the Eucharist as the focus of our life in God and in his church. One youngster, a bit older than the rest (about nine months), sat cross-legged in the very center, with his eyes fixed intently on my face. After the blessing for the fathers and mothers, the ritual calls for a prayer over all present. The ending reads: "May he send his peace upon all who are gathered here, in Christ Jesus our Lord." None of the adults responded. But almost immediately from the mouth of the nine-month-old boy in the middle came a clear and distinct "Amen."

I stared at the child in absolute amazement and so did the parents and some others. After a moment absorbing what had just happened, I said to the assembly: "This is quite extraordinary. I would say that God has arranged something special for this young lad." Since then, with each baptism I perform, I wonder what God hopes for in the future for each child he has just adopted.

Does this incident not remind us of the words of Simeon when the child Jesus, forty days after birth, was brought to the temple by Mary and Joseph as was required by the law of Moses? Simeon prophesied: "This child is destined for the falling and the rising of many in Israel, and to be a sign that will be opposed so that the inner thoughts of many will be revealed—and a sword will pierce your own soul too" (Luke 2:34–35). Can we not also suppose that God has a definitive plan for each of his adopted children who is "presented in the Temple" at the time of baptism?

When Christian parents bring their child to "the temple of the Lord" for baptism, there is the understanding that the newly born belongs to God and through baptism becomes a child of God, a member of the church. Also, freed from original sin, the new Christian will be eligible to receive the inheritance of eternal life in the kingdom of heaven. Parents understand that, but they also wonder what God will expect from the future adult. Indeed, there are parents who do not realize how much will depend on themselves. Unfortunately, instead of guiding and supporting their children toward the fulfillment of God's will, some want their children to be the embodiment of their own unfulfilled dreams.

Most of us were carried at a tender age to the font of baptism. We probably have no idea what our parents may have thought would be God's plan for us. Indeed, at this time in our lives we may be confident that we have fulfilled his overall design for us. We may also remember moments of unfaithfulness, when we pursued interests contrary to the divine will. However, our concern now is only what lies ahead. Our first "amen" may have been uttered long after our baptism and indeed even after our confirmation. At some point we did say "Amen, Lord," and the divine promises are still in place.

Sainthood is a noble ambition.

Before his Ascension into heaven, Jesus assured the apostles that he was going to prepare a place for them in the kingdom of heaven. He also indicated that there are many mansions there, perhaps to let us know that everyone is not equal in their intimacy with the Blessed Trinity. We have not been promised equal status. Mary, the Immaculate Mother of Jesus and our mother, enjoys the highest place. After all, she is the queen of angels and saints. However, our love will be truly full according to our respective capacities. Nor shall we envy those on a "higher" plane. After all, in eternity we will finally understand our status as redeemed and repentant sinners.

We sometimes read in holy writings that there were those who set out to become saints at an early age, often inspired by tales that a pious parent told them. Their ambition was not just to get to heaven.

They wanted to become holy. Ignatius of Loyola, a soldier and aristocrat, decided to pursue holiness while reading the lives of saints during his convalescence from a battle wound. "Why not me, too?" he asked himself.

Of course, such ambition must be considered a good thing. We are supposed to go wherever our talents from God direct us, to become the best that we possibly can be, in accord with his will and commandments. He certainly wills that we reach holiness, which is simply *living for God so he can love us.* His love for us, as is the case of all love, is limited only if our goals are motivated by personal satisfaction and glory. That would not be acceptable.

My suspicion has always been that when young people aspire to sainthood they really want to gain fame, not in the future but while they are alive. Would they be content to be unknown now and attain holy celebrity only after death? More than likely, however, the reality is that they often think it would be adventurous to be famously holy and, indeed, perhaps even fun to be a saint. Adventurous, yes! Fun? Definitely not!

Jesus gave us a warning from the very beginning. When the mother of James and John said to him: "Declare that these two sons of mine will sit, one at your right hand and one at your left, in your kingdom," Jesus asked them: "Are you able to drink the cup that I am about to drink?" They assured him that they could. His response is for us to ponder: "You will indeed drink my cup, but to sit at my right hand and at my left, this is not mine to grant, but it is for those for whom it has been prepared by my Father" (Matthew 20:21–23).

To become a saint, even a lower-case one perhaps known only to God, we must make a generous response to the divine grace and gifts that we receive. He will inspire us to do the good that he expects of us. In a word, we must listen to the voice of the Spirit and then be faithful. Our very ability to speak with God in prayer demands a generous response to the challenges he offers to us. To become a saint that the church will recognize as a fitting example for all demands the practice of heroic charity, which God will confirm by miracles after our death. If God wills it, we will have every opportunity and the accompanying grace. Our problem is that we often fall short of being heroic. Unfortunately, many of us become content just to get to heaven.

To blossom where we are planted

Holiness calls for the fulfillment of God's will every day in every circumstance. During our time as young adults, we make a determination as to how we will spend our lives, what will be our state of life. For most, that is marriage, where our position as husband or wife, father or mother, will be the foundation and instrument of our holiness. Others, however, feel called to sanctity in the choice of a dedicated single life in the service of family, church or community. Often personal or social circumstances lead them to this determination. Among these we may include anyone who responds to a divine call to serve the church as priest or religious.

Yet there are some for whom the single life is not an option, but a foregone conclusion. This happens because of a physical, emotional or mental inability that would put out of the question a complete and free commitment to another person in marriage. For a few there is even the unusual burden of family or community responsibility that arises from special circumstances. No one, however, is beyond the call to holiness. Wherever God's will places us provides every opportunity to become holy.

In addition to our call to a particular way of life, we may have decided on a specialized profession or trade, how we will earn our living. Yet to none of these can we attribute the word *holy,* but only to our state as married or single, priest and/or religious. We will all be either holy men or holy women. In marriage it will be holy husbands or holy wives, holy fathers or holy mothers. Our holiness should, of course, accompany us to the workplace and into our relationship with colleagues, but we will not be saints because we are holy farmers or secretaries, holy teachers or lawyers, holy engineers or financial advisors and so on. Nor can we speak of holy preachers or pastors, holy chaplains or hospital administrators, etc. We may properly speak only about holy priests and holy religious.

It might seem that some Christians have an advantage over others in the pursuit of holiness. Is there a benefit that accrues to those baptized in infancy? We might say so only in the sense that one's family has provided a firm spiritual foundation. On the other hand, a person who struggles against the pressures of a bad moral environment and has determined to be a faithful Christian will have more opportunity than most to practice heroic charity. In that sense everything balances out. There is merit and some wisdom in the saying that only a person who has the opportunity to become a great sinner can truly become a great saint. Conversely, even some with every advantage of early formation in the love of God have in later life betrayed Jesus. It all comes down to personal generosity and the cooperation with grace.

Is the call to religious life or the priesthood an advantage? Such a call provides great opportunities and is often protected from the distractions that surround family life in a society that seems interested only in personal gratification. Yet religious and priests live with the constant challenge to be faithful to a lifestyle that is countercultural and reflects the eternal Jerusalem. They have the constant need to develop the supernatural motives needed to be faithful to Christ in their service of God and his people. Fidelity to the will of God remains the foundation of holiness in whatever state one has been called. Each has its own grace, but especially do marriage and priesthood since each is conferred by a special sacrament. They have some advantage even over religious life, which was not established by Christ, but by the church.

One size gospel fits all.

Those whom God calls to religious life begin their special journey with Jesus on the day of profession when they promise by vow to live the traditional gospel counsels of poverty, chastity and obedience in the service of the church. They accept without reservation the surrender of marriage, property ownership, their choice of work and their place of residence. Their individuality will be limited by the will of another for the good of the community or congregation to which they belong. This they do for the glory of God and the service of the kingdom of heaven.

All Christians, however, are called to live these gospel counsels, namely, to be chaste, to be poor in spirit and always to be ready to serve those in need. Unfortunately, most think that only religious consecrate these virtues by vow. Obviously, the form by which these vows are lived, namely, in a celibate community, is unique. Yet, another form exists which is lived by the vast majority of Christians. Few think about it, but those men and women who enter into Christian marriage also vow poverty, chastity and obedience. The form of their lifelong commitment consists in a sexual bonding for the purpose of mutual support and the raising of a family. By the vows they make in the marriage ceremony, the couple promises fidelity, a sharing of goods and submission to each other in their mutual responsibilities as mother and father. Both religious life and marriage have holiness as their ultimate goal.

A priest of some local fame, known to be a very able preacher and pastor, directed a very successful parish program of religious education for many years. He was also gifted as a musician and liturgist. His parishioners held him in high esteem, and he received his share of praise for his accomplishments. Yet he admitted very frankly that he cherished one compliment more than any other.

His favorite came from a wife and mother to whom he had offered some spiritual guidance in a difficult period of her marriage. She was one of his parishioners, but he had never spoken with her personally before. After a session with her alone and then with both her and her husband, their marriage was restored to its prior bliss. Eventually, she sent him a letter of thanks. In it she wrote: "You would have made a wonderful husband and a great father. But I thank God that he called you to be a priest."

This bears out the wise observation of a seminary professor who always maintained that he would recommend for the priesthood only those men who had the character and determination needed to be a very good husband and father. The virtues required for both are the same, namely, understanding, dedication, generosity and compassion. The grace of ordination will assure that a good man becomes a great priest. Likewise, the grace of matrimony will make a good Christian man a great husband and father. Conversely, the same applies to a Christian woman who seeks holiness as a wife and mother.

In the nature of things spiritual, priesthood and marriage are not incompatible. However, the church has determined that her priests will be celibate, so as to imitate Christ as Bridegroom of the church. Thus a priest best fulfills his own call to holiness when the focus of his love is intimately directed only to the people he serves.

A direct comparison can be made, however, between religious life and marriage, since they are Christian forms of life that by nature are exclusionary. Celibacy, together with the community life of those so vowed, makes the distinction apparent. Yet, their pathways to holiness are linked in the identity they have with the gospel counsels themselves, acknowledged by tradition to be the aforementioned poverty, chastity and obedience. The gospel counsels, consecrated by vow, are applicable to both religious and married couples. In reality married life often reflects more realistically a gospel reality than that which is found in the structured forms of religious life. Marriage provides opportunities on a day-to-day basis to share one's own time and material goods (poverty), to be faithful toward one's committed love (chastity) and to surrender the inclinations of one's own will for the sake of others, one's spouse and children (obedience). In both instances the reality depends on the generosity of the individuals.

The ritual formula used in a marriage ceremony can sound too much like a legal contract and not a life-long spiritual covenant. It would if it contained more expressly the elements of the gospel counsels. The present formula, however, does imply them. It reads: "I take you to be my wife/husband. I promise to be true to you in good times and in bad (chastity), in sickness and in health (poverty). I will love you and honor you all the days of my life (obedience)."

Without changing the present formula, the following might serve as an introduction to be recited in unison:

> I vow and promise to Almighty God, in the presence of God's people and with the full freedom of my will, to take this woman/man (name) as my husband/wife, forsaking all others, that we may become two in one flesh according to the plan of God from the beginning, to remain together as long as both of us shall live, to share our fortunes and all possessions, honoring and accepting each other in every way as equals before God, by the

submission of our wills to support each other and our children, if God blesses us with the family we desire. Let this be known to all, that we are united before God as husband and wife to support each other in our journey together toward eternal life. Therefore, (said separately) I take you (name) to be my wife/husband, and so on.

Jesus our constant companion

On whatever specific path we tread to the ideal of a holy life, living the gospel counsels as religious, priest, married couples or single laity, we do not expect a simple stroll. Even to attain ordinary holiness, that is, be someone who remains loyal to Jesus and does not go over to "the other side," calls for spiritual toughness. Love does not stand still. One either feeds the fire of love, or it goes out. To be sure, the Gospel is very clear. "If any want to become my followers, let them deny themselves and take up their cross daily and follow me" (Luke 9:23).

Saints are not content to follow Jesus, however, but they do the very best to "catch up" and walk along with him as companions. Their concern is to focus on Jesus himself and not on any benefit to themselves. They are not distracted by any reputation they might leave behind after death. In fact, most saints in heaven are unknown to the church at large, with no date on the church's calendar or any place where they are celebrated by the faithful. The church herself recognizes this deficiency on the first day of November with a feast to honor all "those who made it." The following day she remembers those saints "who are waiting at the door," so to speak. Hence on two successive days, as the "church militant" (still struggling) we recognize our union with the "church triumphant" and the "church suffering," that is, in our oneness with Jesus, which we call "the communion of saints." Each one attained the goal because of loyalty to Jesus through the hard times they shared with him. We take comfort in the fact that they have all been through what we now endure.

On November 2 we pray for our loved ones who still await their eternal glory among the souls in purgatory, the faithful departed. We do this "just in case" even for those whom we were inclined to celebrate on All Saints' Day. We all have known some special "saints" who were part of our lives and we know must be in heaven. A saint is, after all, someone who has lived a life in the presence of God and totally for God.

As we remember and honor the saintly parents, priests, teachers or friends who have gone before us, we need to ask ourselves: "Am I ready to be included in this august company?" "Do I have any doubts about my present spiritual condition?" "Am I too busy with my responsibilities?" "Have I forgotten that it is not what I do that pleases our Father in heaven, but that what I do conforms to his will for my life?" And even when I am sure that what I do is exactly what God expects of me, do I take too much credit for my successes or become annoyed if my efforts are not recognized? I could be doing the right things but losing out because I do not have the glory of God as my primary motive. Have I disconnected from Jesus and perhaps laid down the cross that I once took up so eagerly when he beckoned me to follow him?

There are stories about Pope John XXIII, whom the

church has already given the title of Blessed, which illustrate his focus on Jesus that is required of us all, to remember that Jesus is with us at all times. Some anecdotes that have survived are probably myth. One story, however, does have the ring of truth to it. It shows that Pope John always lived in the presence of Jesus, an essential ingredient for true holiness.

In his office where he received visitors and at every table where he held a meeting, there was one special chair, somewhat different from all the rest, simple but distinctive. It was always left unoccupied. Once as a group of bishops were assembling, a new bishop sat in that special chair. Pope John gently reminded him: "Please take another place. Jesus sits there." "For where two or three are gathered in my name, I am there among them" (Matthew 18:20).

All of us should expect that November 1 some day might be our festival, too. We only need to be sure that whatever we do conforms to the will of God (obedience being the first expression of *faith*). Then we must learn in every situation to *trust* in God's purposes, however difficult to reconcile with his goodness. Nor can we expect to understand anything unless we reflect frequently on the words of Jesus and contemplate his works in the New Testament.

We grow to *love* Jesus the more that we serve those who share with us the life and work of the church. Our strength will come from a close association with him through the sacrifice of the Mass, the time we spend before the Blessed Sacrament and wherever we are conscious of the presence of God. Then we will gladly take up our cross and follow him as he trudges to Calvary. We will eventually join him in glory together with the Blessed Virgin Mary and all the saints in the resurrection on the last day.

Only a modified pessimism makes sense.

With all the pressures of the human condition in the various fields of competition, only the rare man or woman can maintain a balanced view of life all the time. Christians who have their eyes on the life to come can remain calm because their attention looks beyond the present day into eternity. We are counting on the clear promise of Jesus to share in the glory of the Resurrection precisely because of the difficult times we endure in this life for the glory of his name (*cf.* Romans 6). So ultimately, a Christian is an optimist. "Be steadfast. All will be well," we say to ourselves.

But in another sense Christians must also be pessimists. How can we be otherwise when we give thought to the words of Jesus: "and you will be hated by all because of my name" (Matthew 10:22). Again, "Those who find their life will lose it, and those who lose their life for my sake will find it" (Matthew 10:39). Even when Jesus speaks of the last days: "But before all this occurs, they will arrest you and persecute you; they will hand you over to synagogues and prisons, and you will be brought before kings and governors because of my name.... You will be betrayed even by parents and brothers, by relatives and friends; and they will put some of you to death" (Luke 21:12, 16). We can never say that Jesus has not warned us.

We are not speaking, of course, about a pessimism that is absolute, a condition that looks for everything to go wrong. Christian pessimism is modified by trust, which always allows for the expectation that sometimes something great will happen, because at times God arranges just that. But we should not expect it too often. If things start to go right all the time, it would mean that God does not trust us anymore, that only if he takes good care of us will we serve him. God does not always take good care of those who serve him well, not on earth anyway.

I once heard of a philosophy professor in an eminent university who had a touch of Nietzsche in him. He was known to expect that every day would bring some keen disappointment. To put it mildly, he always looked on the dark side of life. One day a colleague was surprised to see him in the school corridor with a big smile on his face in place of the usual frown. "What's up?" he asked. "Why do you look so happy?" "Because," was the enthusiastic reply, "*everything* is going wrong today."

Should the professor's attitude surprise us? After all, aren't all of us happy when things turn out just as we expected?

On our journey toward holiness and the kingdom of heaven should we not also be a bit pessimistic, always expecting that our life will be difficult? When you think about it, good Christians are truly happy pessimists, because we are never disappointed. We expect that things might not work out, since God has promised us a lot of difficult times. But we know, too, that we have a God of love and compassion. Thus when a Christian pessimist sees that something is working out for the good, he is ecstatic and praises God.

Not so the optimist. He expects things always to go right and is often disappointed, since many things do not work out to his satisfaction. When things do end up as he expected, he can feel only some satisfaction. An optimist never knows the ecstasy that comes from surprises.

But as Christians with the proper touch of pessimism, we are able to experience ecstasy. We believe that Jesus allows us to share his cross and so are not disappointed when he does. Yet at the same time we also believe in his love for us. Saints know the ecstasy that comes from the surprises of love that is most often experienced in prayer, a sense of bliss that shines in the midst of difficulties. So we, too, can expect that now and then this will happen to us.

We are bound hand and foot.

If we are to be saints, we must seek glory only in Jesus crucified, that is, to share his cross as a sign of divine favor. The image of the Son of God hanging in agony and shame on the cross must remain ever before our eyes to remind us how salvation is won. The cross must dominate the life of every Christian.

"So they took Jesus; and carrying the cross by himself, he went out to what is called the Place of the Skull, which in Hebrew is Golgotha. There they crucified him" (John 19:17–18).

Huge nails were hammered through Jesus' hands and feet to secure him to the cross, as was the custom, although his body was probably supported by ropes or some other way. The great pain can only be imagined. He could not move. After his death a spear opened his side, blood and water together gushing forth to reveal that the heart was broken. Thus we are accustomed to speak of the "five wounds of Jesus." Some chosen souls, the first being Saint Francis of Assisi, have received on their bodies these five painful marks of Jesus' passion (called the stigmata).

One of the saints most recently canonized, Saint Pio of Pietrelcina, for most of his adult life bore the painful wounds of Jesus in his side, in his hands and in his feet. The truth is that this "gift" was not the reason for his glorification by the church. You might say that it was in spite of it, since it caused him to be subject to psychological second-guessing. The stigmata brought fame but also opened the door to misunderstandings and false accusations. All was borne in patient silence, with the daily fatigue in hearing confessions of the countless persons who came to see him. These were the key to his sanctity. He shared the cross of Jesus as he was asked, and he willingly showed the mercy of Jesus to all over a long period of years.

The *external* manifestation of the wounds of Jesus on the body of some saints was given for God's own special reasons. We can only speculate what these reasons might be. But we need not doubt the truth that we all are called to be one with Jesus crucified, to allow our hands, feet and side to experience the *interior* stigmata, to suffer the inconvenience of our hands bound by the spirit of poverty, our feet secured by the bonds of obedience and our heart constrained by chastity, so that we are free to serve our brothers and sisters in every way that love requires and to know that such love is often unrequited.

Let us reflect for a moment on how much we might take the use of our hands and feet for granted, if we are fortunate to be able to do things and to go places as we wish. Those who are in training to take care of the severely handicapped, for example, are sometimes sensitized with a special exercise. They are required to spend a whole day with their hands covered with bags or tied behind their back, or with their feet tied together. They are forced to ask someone's help for the most fundamental personal needs in order to appreciate the emotions and difficulties of the people they care for.

Our hands also can be used to do things that are good or bad, altruistic or selfish. Our feet can take us to places where we plan to do good deeds, or we can intend to do harm. Indeed, there are people who cannot do good or evil since their hands are crippled by severe arthritis, or they cannot walk because of a stroke. They can only think and desire good or evil. Then again, the pain from a broken heart is often more wretched than physical pain.

It is a great gift to be blessed with two functioning hands for work and with feet that can carry us wherever we want. Also, when our hearts are full of joy rather than sorrow—that makes everything wonderful. Looking closer, however, we find that the hands and feet of love are always "nailed" to the responsibilities to which we are called by love itself. Also, the heart full of love will eventually know pain. So by renouncing our own interests, all of us have become crucified with Christ. Love has secured our hands and feet to the will of God, and love has pierced the heart.

It would be presumptuous for anyone to seek the stigmata and its consequent fame, unless one's primary desire is to suffer the pain involved whether or not there were external signs. However, maybe we need not ask, because we already have the invisible stigmata.

The five wounds of Christ belong to all the baptized. We have accepted that our feet be nailed by going only where God directs us, that our hands be fastened by the good we do for our neighbor and that our hearts be pierced by love. We say yes to our crucifixion, even when we would like to remove the nails.

Ready to proceed

The beginning of our study has been a review of the proper attitude and the basic conditions that are required to attain sanctity. Otherwise, the goal is out of reach. It is possible to lose our direction because of false notions. With integrity of purpose, however, and the grace of God, we can successfully pursue our intention to become holy.

Our first need is to recognize that a saint's vocation is love. Without the proper concept, for instance, of what love really means there is no progress, because the struggle to love may get focused on oneself. Love is not a matter of feeling holy, but of a total surrender of oneself to God and his will. We learn that such love will constantly be tested, because it is based on trust of the beloved. We will need the humility to accept the person we love as he is and not try to form him in our image. Jesus is not always whom he appears to be at first sight.

We must not set the conditions of love. That is up to God, who loved us first. Our love is a response to his. The Father determines what our life will be, having created us freely and called us as one of his children.

He does not love us separately from the others whom he has adopted through baptism. We pursue holiness within the church as the one Body of Christ, recognizing that the Father requires us to journey together into the eternal kingdom.

This pursuit of holiness must be the all-encompassing passion that will place in proper perspective everything else we do and every person we deal with, whether family, close friends or mere acquaintances and even enemies. We must also be conscious of God's plan for bringing others to the possession of eternal life. None of us is in competition.

Also, we will become saints only where God has planted us, in the state of life to which we are called. Otherwise we have pursued our own will from the beginning. That choice itself, whether of marriage, priesthood, religious life or the single lay state dedicated to charity, is the inspiration of God. Then his grace will accompany us at the moments we are in need of it, not to be afraid of any difficulty and to overcome our innate self-love that might interfere in the fulfillment of his plan. It is also important to thank God for all the people he has placed in our lives, recognizing that each one is part of his overall plan to guide us. To ignore any of them might be to discountenance one of his messengers. Then we will always be aware that everyone is important to him.

Finally, holiness is the proper fulfillment of our redeemed nature and is thus intimately connected with the Passion of Jesus. The shadow of the cross of Calvary, upon which the Son of God died, remains the sign of God's love. It is necessarily reflected in every Christian gathering or endeavor. To be drawn through Jesus into the life of the Triune God, which is holiness, there can be no illusion about the need to embrace Jesus on the cross. A few are called to suffer physical pain like his. But all will join in his sufferings in some way, through fatigue from labor, through misunderstandings, through failure, or through false accusations, to name a few possibilities. There is no other way to be close to Jesus. He is the source of our strength to endure, not the source of physical comfort. Sainthood will never be a rose garden.

Sanctity is the practice of an art based on the spiritual science found throughout the Scriptures, both Old and New Testaments. We learn most, of course, from the Gospels, since they deal most directly with Jesus, the object of our affection and holiness itself, for he is the Way, the Truth and the Life. Like any science, sanctity demands a respect for the rules that are inherent to its nature. Hence, we move on to ponder those practices, attitudes and expectations so intrinsic to sainthood that without their being in place progress in holiness is impossible.

CHAPTER TWO

the ground rules

And this is eternal life; that they may know
you, the only true God, and Jesus Christ
whom you have sent.
—John 17:3

I n any worldly endeavor basic circumstances and appropriate steps are required to make progress toward an expected conclusion. They are just as necessary in the development of the spiritual life. What drives one toward success in every human activity is also required in the pursuit of sanctity.

Our goal is to reach an intimate union with the Triune God. In the call to holiness we recognize that the impetus of grace will come first from the Holy Spirit, whose special gifts we receive through the sacrament of confirmation. These are named for the powers they confer, namely, wisdom, understanding, knowledge, fortitude, counsel, piety and fear of the Lord.

The first task is to look into our lives and make sure that three conditions for holiness are in place. They can be compared to the requirements needed for growth in the plant kingdom. Once we have the seed in hand (grace), we still require sunlight (prayer), good soil (humility) and water (a generous spirit). We then turn to the fundamental spiritual principles found in the Sermon on the Mount that will guide us toward holiness. These beatitudes from the lips of Jesus are considered a summary of the gospel life and properly reflect the faithful use of the Gifts of the Holy Spirit.

Rule 1: Listen up!

Since love is at the core of holiness, it stands to reason that direct contact is the first condition for the journey. After all, we can only love a person with whom we are in touch, speak with frequently and listen to attentively. Otherwise true intimacy with the one who wants to love us is not possible.

To love Jesus demands that we talk with him and listen to him, learn how to pray effectively. Yet our bond with Jesus is so personal and special that we can only be given general guidance. Our success will depend on Jesus himself, who will ask the Spirit to give us the gift of prayer. The process of preparing ourselves for the full impulse of the Spirit may be a lifetime in developing. But there must be a steady process from verbal prayers of petition or thanksgiving to the infused prayer of contemplation itself.

For the most part this calls for a willingness to become an attentive listener. Unfortunately, beginners in the art of prayer place a lot of importance on the amount of talking they do, as well as the amount of time they invest in prayer. But progress is made only when the mouth begins to do less and the ears of the spirit tune in to the voice of God.

To hear God speak demands silence, since he speaks to the heart. He cannot be heard amid distractions and noise and even over the sound of one's own voice. When we turn our minds to God, we must remember that we are speaking with three Divine Persons, who are each distinct and yet are the one God. We do not pray to the Father separated from the Son and the Holy Spirit. As in the perfect prayer of God's people, the eucharistic sacrifice of the Mass, all prayer is directed *to* the Father, *together with* the Son, who leads us to the Father, and *united with* all God's people by the power of the Holy Spirit.

Early on I learned that some very devout and good people spend a lifetime "saying prayers" rather than praying. One such asked me the following question: "Father, I promised to make a novena to Saint Anthony in thanksgiving for a favor I received. But I forgot to say the prayers one day. Do I have to start all over again?"

I resisted the temptation to give a dissertation on novenas. "A novena is a private devotion," I replied. "So you are the one who makes the rules. You will have to answer your own question."

Another was an elderly woman who had a conscience problem. She had over the course of her eighty-five years managed to collect a fistful of holy cards, each one of which contained a prayer that she had promised at different times in her life to recite each night before she retired. She asked me: "Almost every night now I fall asleep before I have finished them. Is God displeased with me for not fulfilling my promises?"

I told her not to be concerned, because God under-stands her condition. I urged her to come in again, bring me all the cards she had, and we would talk some more. The following Sunday she came to the sac-risty and showed me the cards. I counted forty-two, all very much used.

"You must have a favorite," I suggested. "Which is it?" She shuffled through them and took out a picture of the Sacred Heart of Jesus and showed me the prayer on the back. "Well," I said, "I now declare with all the power I have from the church that you are no longer required to recite these prayers each night. You are absolved of your promises. If you wish, recite this prayer to the Sacred Heart of Jesus each night, but no others."

She allowed me to keep the remaining cards and left very relieved and pleased. The next day, having looked at each card and marveled at the woman's obvious sense of deep piety, I prayed for some mod-icum of her fidelity to God. Through the years I have often been inspired by the elderly people who are reaching the end of a spiritually fruitful life and are very much in touch with the God they will soon meet.

Prayer should not be complicated. It is a sit-down with someone we love and who loves us. Basically it is simple conversation, with few words and a lot of silence so as to enjoy each other's company.

Rule 2: Be Honest With Yourself.

The second condition needed to attain holiness is to recognize the truth about oneself. Love is possible only when those involved are accepting of each other and want to give to the other rather than benefit personally from the relationship. God, of course, cannot learn anything from us and the only things we can give him are glory, praise and thanksgiving. It is not our call to convince God how good we are and how much we deserve his love. Rather we need to appreciate that God loves us in spite of ourselves and be ever grateful.

Would-be saints often find themselves on a plateau, feeling close to God but never having that constant sense of joy and tranquility that reflects true peace. We can be detoured on the journey to holiness by a false notion of who we are in relationship to God and our neighbor. We must remember that progress depends on knowing the truth about ourselves as God knows us and not living a lie.

Our tendency is not to reveal the unfavorable side of our character, especially to those we want to admire us. We do it most often to save face, lest others know the less-than-perfect person behind the pleasant smile. Perhaps some things we even lie to ourselves about. Saints, of course, try to be open about their weakness and limitations and are not afraid that others will think less of them than they appear. They realize that Jesus knows all about them anyway, so why bluff. Holiness makes us that way.

One time I witnessed an example of such honesty. A good friend had expressed a confusing political opinion to a crowd of fellow workers, and I watched their silent acceptance of his view. His manner was convincing. When we were alone, I commented to him, "Bill, you are such a phony!"

He smiled and replied, "You know me better than you think."

Most of us would become defensive if our sincerity were questioned like that. Indeed, after that experience I learned to define sanctity as the quality of being totally honest with God and within oneself. In other words, a saint is not a phony.

As children, we probably heard the sage advice of a parent, guardian or teacher that we should always stand on our own two feet. "Don't be concerned about what others think of you. Do what you know is right. You will feel better about it in the long run." But we were usually more worried about the *short* run. Peer pressure, being accepted as "one of the crowd," often outweighed the "right thing."

Unfortunately, because of sin and a sinner's inherent pride, our usual concern is that no one should really know us as we are, with all our duplicity. To fear the harsh judgment of another, which is called human respect, is a common weakness that afflicts adults more than children, although for more complicated reasons. Job security is one example. We often sacrifice our dignity and at times even our loyalty to Jesus, in order to be liked, or to be respected, or to be thought of as a nice person, even by people of whom we are not really fond.

We might also be harsh with someone with whom we disagree, which violates Christian charity. A saint tries to listen with patience to another person's point of view so as to give a response that reflects understanding. However, to hide our disagreement in order to remain popular is a simple case of hypocrisy. I like to call it "being a phony."

Also to pass the buck rather than make an unpopular decision, to let someone else be the bad guy, is at best cowardly. I once heard a child say: "My father never lets me do anything." When questioned, he admitted that his mother never refused him anything. It seems she always said "yes" when she knew the father's answer would be "yes," but "ask your father" when she knew the answer had to be "no."

As in all things, Jesus is our example here, too. In Matthew 22:16 we find the Pharisees giving Jesus a compliment, which should make us pause: "Teacher, we know that you are sincere and teach the way of God in accordance with the truth, and show deference to no one; for you do not regard people with partiality." So, how do we handle questions that are asked about particular people or a request to give one's opinion? We should evade as courteously as possible a "nosy" question. Nevertheless, everyone who has a right to know the truth must be given the truth. To deny, even by evasion, a truthful answer to a legitimate question that someone has a right to ask is to lie. And to give an answer which would please, but which is false, is a double lie.

The Father has sent us Jesus who is the Way, the *Truth* and the Life. Hence, all of us, especially parents, teachers, priests and bishops, are required by the rules of holiness to guide toward the truth those who depend on the church to teach them the ways of God. Should we fail through human respect, we will begin to deny the truth to ourselves. We will even distort the word of God in the Scriptures and accept only what our personal lives will find comfortable. This becomes especially egregious when it affects the truth that we are obliged to teach as parents or teachers. This would be a gross dishonesty.

Saints learn to see themselves as they are in the sight of God. They make no pretenses in relating to others but depend on Jesus to show them their real selves. They know that he will always tell the truth even if we will not like him anymore. He is not a phony.

Rule 3: Forget about feeling holy.

We might put that another way. Holiness is more than doing "holy" things so that we can feel good. True charity toward everyone can sometimes make us feel uncomfortable, but the exercise of love remains the essence of sanctity. Yet, it is possible to do the right thing for the wrong reason or the wrong thing for a good reason, in order to feel good. Neither one qualifies as a virtue. We need to learn to do the right thing even when it proves costly to our comfort or prestige. At times the less holy of two courses of action is the one to choose in order to do the right thing. There is no other way to holiness.

I learned that powerful lesson from a young lady of nine years during my first years as a priest. The memory still humbles me. I was teaching a religious education class for youngsters preparing for First Holy Communion. The girl had done better than all the rest in the final examination, even after a late start. As I had promised the class, there was a prize for top honors. A choice was offered. She might choose either a nine-inch-tall statue of the Blessed Mother and the infant Jesus or a bag of caramel candies, easily five pounds. She hesitated briefly and reached for the candies.

Visibly disappointed that my student had failed to learn a sense of values along with her lessons, I picked up the statue, studied it and looked wistfully at the girl: "You don't like the statue, Jennifer?"

"Oh yes, Father, it's just beautiful," was the simple reply.

"Then why did you choose the candy?" I asked.

She looked straight into my eyes. "Well," said Jennifer, "I can share the caramels with my friends."

I gasped and almost cried. She understood goodness only too well.

Was young Jennifer an exception to the accepted wisdom that children are very self-centered? Why do we pick on children even though, because of the original sin, all of us are selfish? The lifetime struggle to learn to love, which is the opposite of self-centeredness (or self-love), does indeed begin when we are children. Jennifer, no doubt, had the example of two very hard-working parents, and she knew that they loved her. She was luckier than many.

Selfishness, which is an expression of spiritual and often emotional immaturity, is the foremost reason for the break-up of friendships, marriages, business partnerships and other relationships less personal. It is also the enemy of holiness. When selfish people perceive a threat to their self-importance or personal fulfillment, they get defensive and lash out even against those whom they claim to love and respect. Unless acknowledged, selfishness always gets worse and brings destruction in its wake.

After these many years, how do we rate on the selfishness scale? Do we still at times prefer to do the holy thing, with a certain degree of self-righteousness, rather than the right thing? Undoubtedly we have begun to recognize some truth about ourselves and to acknowledge our limitations. Yet even with the steady growth in emotional and spiritual maturity, pride is always just beneath the surface.

Indeed, we might feel that it is difficult to be humble when everyone around us is so incompetent, lazy or just plain inconsiderate. But before limiting our generosity in defense, we need to remember the words of Jesus: "It will not be so among you; but whoever wishes to be great among you must be your servant" (Matthew 20:26). Also, we can be sure that Jesus will be pleased if we do not hold back our joy when we experience his gifts to others. We need to learn, as Jennifer did, to share our happiness with others.

Rule 4: Forgive ahead of time.

All of us have been redeemed from sin by the death of Jesus, and we live in total dependence on God's mercy. Our difficulty as self-centered sinners is the need to forgive others just as our heavenly Father forgives us.

With the power of the Holy Spirit's gift of *counsel*, however, we will be able to exercise the virtue of prudence in our dealings with the people and circumstances that affect our lives. We will give the benefit of the doubt in the assessment of motives in order to forgive others ahead of time. We will be strengthened by what Jesus assured us: "Blessed are the merciful, for they will receive mercy" (Matthew 5:7).

A consciousness of our own need of mercy will have a twofold effect. We will routinely live a life of penance to atone for our past sinfulness. We will practice mortification to strengthen us against temptations that are always near the surface, especially toward rash judgments and moral superiority. Thus we will develop a balanced outlook toward our fellow sinners and come to know that any offense against us, however blatant, is even a more serious offense against God, our creator. If he is ready to forgive, so must we be. How we forgive others is the gauge our heavenly Father uses in offering forgiveness to us.

Our judgment of others is easily influenced negatively by a lifestyle or thought pattern that contradicts our own. We tend to think that, because their actions and thinking are so wrong, nothing that they do can be right. The compassion of our Savior, not personal animosity, must motivate us. We will leave final justice to him. Our joy will focus on our own grace of forgiveness and the good that can exist even in those whose general style of life is in stark contrast to our own.

Jesus has told us to be perfect as our heavenly Father is perfect since he allows the sun to shine on the just and unjust. He sends his rain on the upright and on sinners (*cf.* Matthew 5:44–48). The real test of holiness, therefore, is to reach out with forgiveness to everyone even before mercy is asked for.

Rule 5: Look Jesus in the eye.

Even the worldly-wise know enough to distrust those who avoid direct eye contact when speaking. Some are embarrassed to reveal their true selves, whether that would be their fears and weakness or their outright duplicity. We all believe instinctively that the eyes are the windows of the soul and can reveal the presence of hypocrisy. Whatever the cause, no one has confidence in the downcast or averted look.

When Jesus was calling his disciples, one of the original twelve was Nathanael. Philip told him about Jesus, the prophet from Nazareth. He responded: "Can anything good come out of Nazareth?" (John 1:46).

Upon seeing Nathanael, Jesus said: "Here is truly an Israelite in whom there is no deceit!" (John 1:47). Jesus had extended the height of compliments to this new follower as a man who can be trusted to say what he means and mean what he says. Such a characteristic identifies a person who makes no pretense to be other than what he is. When this involves one's motives, such lack of guile is termed simplicity, which is certainly not simplemindedness. In the spiritual realm, the virtue is called *purity of heart*.

We all start out as moral cowards, because we were born as sinners. With the power of the Holy Spirit's gift of *fortitude*, however, we have our defense against the human respect that makes us timid in the face of moral challenges. Because he considers us his close associates and faithful disciples, Jesus expects us to look him in the eye when we declare that we will be courageous in the face of persecution and patient in the face of ridicule. By our loyal perseverance, we will understand the meaning of the words: "Blessed are the pure in heart, for they will see God" (Matthew 5:8).

If we are unwilling to look Jesus straight in the eyes as he peers down on us from the cross, from beneath that crown of thorns piercing his bloody brow, we will realize that we cannot be trusted, that our motives are selfish, that we are truly cowards. When we are able to look Jesus unflinchingly in the eye we have one proper mark of holiness, *a true Israelite who is without guile.*

Rule 6: Simplify your life.

Basic principles and fundamental skills need to be reviewed if one wishes to make progress in science or the arts, in craftsmanship or sports. Proper conditions must be in place and specific actions are required to attain an expected goal. This applies as well to the divine science and the spiritual art of becoming more and more like Jesus, who has told us: "Take my yoke upon you, and learn from me; for I am gentle and humble in heart" (Matthew 11:29).

Thus we return to the first and indispensable ingredient of sanctity, which is to live humbly. By the power of the Holy Spirit's gift of *understanding,* we are able to know our true self in relation to God. We will place our trust in his continued care that he has shown us from the beginning. This will define our role as servants to each other. Our guide is the declaration of Jesus: "Blessed are the poor in spirit, for theirs is the kingdom of heaven" (Matthew 5:3).

A spiritual person finds the pursuit of wealth for its own sake, strictly for the power and comfort it provides, to be abhorrent. A lifestyle that refuses to share one's material blessings with those less fortunate disturbs any person of good will. It contradicts the basic human instinct for compassion and responsibility. For union with Jesus, however, poverty of spirit touches on more than the mere unholy attachment to possessions, pleasures or social position.

The Christian attitude toward being poor flows from the inherent realization that all I am and have has been given to me by God, beginning with my very life. He expects an accounting of his gifts and how I used them when he returns. This includes both the ordinary and special talents of mind and body.

We only have to look about us to realize that we possess gifts that some others do not. We certainly know other people who possess more talent in particular areas than we do. More importantly, we see that not everyone is born with normal physical or mental competence, or is blessed with a loving family. In some societies many lack any chance for education and social advancement. Also, we must not forget that we would never have arrived at the present moment without the people who took care of us as children. The only credit we might take unto ourselves, to be given lightly, is that we used the gifts God gave us.

Truly humble people are those who recognize these realities. The knowledge of one's own sinfulness, real or possible, is a constant. Hence, the saint praises God each day for his continuing mercy and for the Son who was sent to be one of us and to suffer and die on the cross for our salvation. This carries over into our relationship with all others, to the sharing of our goods, our time and talents, and propels us to respect the dignity of God that dwells in each of God's children.

The most well-known saint in the church's calendar is the one called "the little poor man of Assisi." Men and women of every faith have great interest in Saint Francis, because he did what they would wish they were capable of, namely, to reject the vanities of this world. Throughout history those who renounce the opportunity for fame and fortune in order to become identified with the poor have received the notice of their contemporaries. After more than seven centuries, Francis of Assisi is still an example for all the church.

There may be some who do not know that he lived in thirteenth-century Italy (having died on October 3, 1226). Some may not know that he bore the wounds of Jesus in his body for the last two years of his life. But everyone knows that he was a rich young man who made himself poor for the love of Jesus, Son of God. Like Jesus he wished to share the life of the simple people and to be identified with those on the edges of society. In the beginning of his conversion to his new life, he associated himself with communities of lepers. He embraced their condition of poverty and insignificance.

Of course, poverty in itself is no virtue. Otherwise, all poor people would be saints. What is expected of all would-be saints is to be poor in spirit. This means, first of all, to recognize that all of us have received everything from God, including life, family, talents, opportunities and so forth. In that sense, all of us are poor. Hence the wealth we have attained through the application of his gifts should not be considered totally ours. We use our goods, both spiritual and material, for those toward whom we have responsibility and to be generous to those who, without any fault of their own, are in need.

Francis was motivated to be poor because he was humbled by the thought that the Son of God was born in poverty and then lived the simple life of a man who was dependent on his labor. Those are dependent who have no economic influence, who must work for their own livelihood and who must be satisfied with the simple needs of life. Thus did Christ live and so would Francis. He especially withdrew himself from any exercise of power over others. He wished to be a servant of all.

"Just as the Son of Man came not to be served but to serve, and to give his life a ransom for many" (Matthew 20:28).

The first rule of action for beginners in the quest for holiness is to simplify one's lifestyle as much as possible in accord with the responsibilities of our state of life. Without many distractions our goal comes into remarkable focus. We strengthen our identity with the Son of God, poor and crucified. The road ahead suddenly becomes very clear.

Rule 7: Expect love and tears to mix.

No one becomes holy who is always pursuing the happy life, never wanting to know sadness. Even pagans find that this life is a mixture of love and sorrow. Yet only for those who love God can sorrow be called a blessing, since we remember what Jesus said: "Blessed are those who mourn, for they will be comforted" (Matthew 5:4).

When the heart embraces another person, we know that we must prepare ourselves for sorrow, for at some point the circle of love will be broken, temporarily or permanently. How we handle the separation from a loved one or the sorrow we feel in difficult times will be the gauge of what degree of holiness we have attained. We will experience a more intense sorrow as our love deepens. Only in the life of heaven, where there is no sorrow, can we expect to be fully comforted.

Family life often mixes love with tears, even in Nazareth. Only a mother would appreciate the sorrow of Mary the mother of Jesus, who watched her son grow up within the shadow of the sufferings that she knew awaited him. Not many think of the Virgin Mary as a widow, but she certainly knew sadness and loneliness after Joseph died. Later she shared her son's Passion and death so intimately, as she watched beside the cross, that we honor her with the title "Sorrowful Mother" or, more poignantly, "the Mother of Sorrows."

We have at least two examples from the Gospels of Jesus himself weeping. He cried when he witnessed the sorrows of his friends, Mary and Martha, at the death of their brother (*cf.* John 11:35). He also wept over Jerusalem, as he thought about those who would reject the love he was offering (*cf.* Luke 19:41–44). I am sure that Jesus and Mary themselves shared many tears as mother and son, about which the Gospels are silent. Yet it is easy to picture the scene when Jesus visited his mother to say goodbye before he ascended into heaven, their last embrace until they would be reunited in heaven some twenty years later. Or we can imagine that Jesus wept earlier on, when he left home to begin his public preaching, and then on his last visit before leaving for Jerusalem and his Passion and death.

We cannot really expect to be different from these two holy ones. We remember the tears shared with loved ones in their moments of difficulty. The time for weeping is when we share the sorrow of someone we love, or when we feel the pain that comes from the thought of separation from a loved one. Pain comes when a loved one is torn from our heart by death or distance, and some know the stab to the heart by an act of betrayal. The heart only hurts when it knows love.

Conversely, there are many memories of tears of joy when we were united with loved ones after a separation of some time. These are the moments of our comfort here on earth, and it comes only from those who share a life of love with us. Only one who has never loved does not know how to weep. Self-pity does not count. Since holiness is being in love, saints expect to weep often. Some found the time to weep over their sins and were comforted by the mercy of God.

With the power of the Holy Spirit's gift of *knowledge* we are able to look into the heart of another as God might and to focus our attention only on their good. Our sense of loss becomes subordinate to their interests. Thus each sorrow is a step nearer the absolute surrender to God's will, which is sanctity. We exercise our faith in the Resurrection when a loved one dies and are able to rejoice in the goodness of a loving God, who will give us the comfort he has promised.

Rule 8: Calm down!

The comforting refrain that "man proposes and God disposes" comes to the lips of the faith-filled Christian in response to any change of plan necessitated by an unforeseen happening. We know those who wail in abject disappointment. Others will protest that what they had planned would have brought much good to many. Have not all of us at one time or another heard nominal Christians, at moments of stress, scream in protest that God is not fair? For those whose faith is weak, there is also a bit of cynical advice: To make God smile, give him the details of your plans for the future.

The thing that you did not want to happen may be a temporary sorrow, as heavy rain on the day of the family's long-planned picnic. It could be something more far-reaching as the sudden death of a very important person in one's life. In any case we are forced to make adjustments to our way of living or to plans that have been carefully worked out. Mature people are not given to frustration over circumstances that are beyond their control. Emotionally stable, they know how to cope with disappointment and are able to restructure their lives accordingly.

Spiritual maturity, on the other hand, concerns itself with eternal values and expectations and is prepared in advance for a new manifestation of God's will. Saints are always on the lookout for signs that might indicate what God has arranged for them. Their response to an unforeseen change of a plan that is already in progress is often more like: "Where is God directing me now?" This attitude, however, does not come about by an act of stoic acceptance. With the power of the Holy Spirit's gift that we call "fear of the Lord," we will be able to exercise the virtue of temperance that is fundamentally a control over our sensual and emotional appetites. Our intellectual and spiritual judgments are then able to be truly free, allowing for tranquility of soul. This will be especially important when something happens that calls for a change that will affect the whole course of one's life. These could concern career choices, marriage or something less vital, as whether to move to another city or to another country.

In one form or another we can all tell about "a phone call that changed my life." But no one will ever top the most important visit in the history of human-kind, when an angel of the Lord came to a Virgin of Nazareth in prayer to say the equivalent of: "Now, Mary, before you do another thing, God wants you to consider this." Mary gave a very positive and submissive response to becoming the mother of God when she replied: "Let it be with me according to your word" (Luke 1:38). With her answer she affected the entire future of the world, as well as her own and that of Joseph, her husband. This fulfillment of the divine will had been in the works for hundreds of years, as evident from the testimony of the prophets.

Mary is told about another "heavenly notice" that affected the lives of her elderly relatives Elizabeth and Zachary. In their old age they would be parents of John the Baptist, who would "thirty years hence" leave the desert to proclaim her Son's presence to God's people. From this we should learn for our own lives that every seemingly accidental occurrence is only God's will playing itself out and pray for the understanding and courage to live by it.

For instance, can anyone doubt that at this time, somewhere in the world, a young man is considering a call from God to become a priest, and this young man will become an eventual successor to the current Holy Father, the bishop of Rome? We know that God rarely acts in one grand gesture. For most of us his ultimate will is made known in small steps (like learning to accept disappointments). We are prepared for a more generous response later on when his long-range plan will become evident to us. Unfortunately, he rarely sends an angel. But he does send the Spirit of Wisdom upon those who ask him.

God often guides us by circumstances that are beyond our control. Perhaps he just wants us to slow down, to rely less on our own resources and turn in trust to him. He makes some of us pay attention through a near encounter with death, which never happened because he did not permit it. Indeed, I am firmly convinced that every upset to our well-laid plans is God's way of saying: "Listen up! I have another idea." To put it another way, saints are always alert for God's surprises.

Only saints are in full control of their emotions for or against any person, or in reaction to any circumstances. They are in possession of their lives because they know that God has his reasons for placing them in each circumstance. They are not cowards, but live with filial respect for the divine plan and are fortified by the words of Jesus: "Blessed are the meek, for they will inherit the earth" (Matthew 5:5).

Rule 9: Learn from your troubles.

The Gospel describes Joseph, husband of Mary, as a "just" man. This means that he always sought to do what was right by everyone, especially the Lord God. We are progressing toward sainthood when we can be described as "just" in the same way. We can sense that someone we know is a saint, or not a saint, by his or her response to acts that may be described as unfair. Holiness on earth is more than the state of *being* holy, but rather a state of *doing what is just*. Tempered with mercy, justice must guide a Christian's relationship with people everywhere, whether close to home, far away or all places in between. We leave their deficiencies to the God of mercy, remembering always that the everyday variety of justice is the practice of common courtesy in all circumstances.

With the Holy Spirit's gift of *piety* we are able to exercise our responsibilities to God, especially adoration and obedience, and then focus our energies in treating our fellows in the human family, of whatever age, condition or culture, with the dignity that they have received from God, their creator. Since our intelligent nature accepts only what it perceives as reasonable (even when it is objectively erroneous), our sense of justice will recoil at any decision that is lopsided in favor of the stronger, richer or socially superior person. This holds true even when our personal motive is selfishness. The mind, when unfettered by self-interest, is always right. But there is the difficulty.

The sinful human being often acts contrary to his intelligence or his instincts of justice. When he rebels against what is perceived to be stupid or unfair and is unable to do anything about it, the heart becomes agitated and the soul is disturbed. Reactions are often fatal to the peace that is God's gift to those who want to live in his presence. A saint, of course, does not lose this peace because Christ has warned us to expect injustice as part of life and that there will always be those who will act for personal benefit and against the interests of others. A saint, however, will always rise in defense of others who are being unjustly treated. Indeed, a forceful response in the defense of another is the one time that we can refer to anger as a virtue.

All of us, at times, are victims of unjust acts by a thoughtless or unscrupulous person, even within our own small world. On a broad scale, humanity's cruelty to other humans in every age is well documented and not unknown in our own time. Violence and injustice are the rule in many places. Often the children suffer most from hunger and disease because a powerful person misused civil or military authority.

In many countries immigrant ethnic groups are treated without compassion, often suffering great indignities simply because of who they are. Sometimes very serious injustices result in death. Throughout the centuries people have hungered and thirsted for justice and found that in this world such hunger and thirst were rarely satisfied. However, when such injustices are considered as sharing in those suffered by Christ, as special opportunities to atone for sin, the wisdom of the beatitude will be experienced: "Blessed are those who hunger and thirst for righteousness, for they will be filled" (Matthew 5:6).

Life is not fair. Jesus said as much, and we have his crucifixion as the prime example. Our Christian faith teaches that through injustice, salvation was made possible. The Savior's death on the cross teaches us that only through personal indignities suffered patiently do we grow into the image of Jesus and merit the eternal kingdom of justice. Even the responses to an injustice done against oneself, or others, must be tempered with mercy. Learning that balance is a direct path to holiness. Sainthood, built on prayer and humility, reflects a life of justice and mercy lived in favor of others and produces true peace of soul.

Just to complete the picture: "Blessed are those who are persecuted for righteousness' sake, for theirs is the kingdom of heaven. Blessed are you when people revile you and persecute you and utter all kinds of evil against you falsely on my account. Rejoice and be glad, for your reward is great in heaven" (Matthew 5:10–12).

Rule 10: Stand tall!

Finally, we come to the test that truly measures our progress in the pursuit of sanctity. It concerns the promise that Jesus made to his disciples at the Last Supper and fulfilled after his Resurrection. On the night before he died, he said to the Apostles: "Peace I leave with you; my peace I give to you. I do not give to you as the world gives. Do not let your hearts be troubled, and do not let them be afraid" (John 14:27). After he had risen from the dead, he came among them in the upper room, where they were hiding in fear and greeted them: "Peace be with you" (John 20:19).

When we allow confusion, distrust or fear to rob us of this gift of peace, we have focused on our own self-interest and begin to think in terms of personal defense. On the other hand, the less we are disturbed by the evil around us, the attacks of enemies or the disappointments that life offers at every turn, the closer we have been drawn into the life of the Triune God. Peace is the fruit of the Holy Spirit's gift of wisdom.

A reading of the lives of saints reveals almost universal incidents of false accusations or at least jealous criticisms from close associates. The refusal to be alarmed and to leave all things in the hands of God was the characteristic response. Saints are often seen by some of their less-holy contemporaries as a bit strange because they never get angry or speak harshly about others. With the power of the Holy Spirit's gift of wisdom, they turn away from self-interest and think only of the well-being of *all* God's children, even those who persecute them.

So we come to an undeniable seal of sanctity. "Blessed are the peacemakers, for they will be called children of God" (Matthew 5:9). We will know for certain that we qualify as "children of God" if we are indeed his *instruments of peace* wherever we go. If we have to admit that our presence among family, friends or colleagues is sometimes the cause of division, we can probably acknowledge that we often take a strong stance in disputes and make harsh judgments against other people's actions or point of view. Especially if coupled with a touch of arrogance, such conduct will certainly lack the compassion of Christ and disqualify one as peacemaker.

To spread peace, we must first possess it within ourselves. Nothing will disturb us if we possess the virtue of true charity by which we act with the forbearance of God. He does what is best for each one of his children. Unfortunately, human beings tend to judge what is in someone's best interest in accord with their own fallible judgment.

Then again, some divisions should not be unexpected when they are the result of our fidelity to the teachings of Jesus. For the Savior challenges us: "I came to bring fire to the earth, and how I wish it were already kindled!" (Luke 12:49).

> Do not think that I have come to bring peace to the earth; I have not come to bring peace, but a sword.

For I have come to set a man against his
   father,
a daughter against her mother,
and a daughter-in-law against her
   mother-in-law;
and one's foes will be members of one own's
   household. (Matthew 10:34–36)

Saints who went to their martyrdom are our examples of such fidelity.

We may not become saints by surrendering our bodies to torture and death for the faith, but we are called to be martyrs in our daily lives. We are called to be one with Jesus, which demands that we stand tall alongside him, undisturbed and unafraid in the cause of truth and justice.

CHAPTER THREE

the breath of the spirit

Lord, teach us to pray.
—Luke 11: 1

U
p until now we have been considering the
ideal of holiness as something to be desired, a grace
that can be requested from God. We have reflected on
the goal itself and the attitude required for its pursuit.
Yet we are acutely aware that the fulfillment of our
desire requires more than our good intentions.

The several steps to be taken concern, among
other things, growth in prayer, a deep and personal
knowledge of Jesus, the practice of virtue, conversion
of mind and heart and the pursuit of divine wisdom as
the basis of spiritual joy. Nor is it a matter of perfect-
ing each step before we proceed to the next. All factors
are recycled back and forth and are interconnected
ever deeper as we advance in sanctity, always within
the bosom of the church and in union with Mary, the
mother of Jesus.

What, we ask, is the constant factor in this journey? A comparison may be properly made with the
reality of our physical nature. As we are very well

aware, death comes to the body when it ceases to breathe. The person may be in the prime of life, intellectually brilliant and enjoying a modicum of professional success. But if breath is cut off, all experiences, talents and energy become void. He dies. To a lesser degree, of course, what one might accomplish under healthy conditions is limited by any impairment to one's breathing apparatus through emphysema or other lung disease. A good oxygen supply is essential to life.

Likewise, in a different dimension, the spiritual energy of grace fuels the fulfillment of supernatural powers. The soul must breathe. Hence, insofar as we breathe in the oxygen of God's presence are we lifted up by the Spirit and united to the Father through the Son, made man. Only the breath of the spirit makes possible union with the Triune God, and prayer is the life-breath of sanctity. Only by perseverance in prayer and steady progress in the art of prayer does a life of perfect charity become a realistic goal.

We need to understand prayer, its purpose and how we direct our spiritual energies by the power of the Spirit through prayer. Then we keep our interior life free of any confusion that might arise because of our own self-centered fancies about holiness.

Prayer is a two-way street.

Excuse me if I use an illustration from the secular world of sports to illustrate the simple but essential fact that prayer must be directed to God primarily for his glory, not only for our own good.

The inimitable Yogi Berra, Hall of Fame catcher for the New York Yankees, is credited with some great sayings, and many betray a profound wisdom about life and at times a deep sense of the spiritual. My favorite concerns the game of baseball itself. In the bottom of the ninth inning in a close contest, with the winning runs on base, the opposition batter swung and missed a second strike. He stepped away. Before stepping back into the batter's box, he made the Sign of the Cross on himself and with his bat traced a cross in the dirt near the plate. Yogi got up from his crouch, strode forward and rubbed out the cross with the tip of his spiked shoe. He stared at the batter and said very firmly, "Why don't we just let God watch the game?"

Did Yogi think that God might take sides if he were asked? I rather think that he was more annoyed by the public display of piety than anything else. If the batter strikes out, religion gets a bad name. And what if the pitcher himself was also asking the Almighty for the favor of a third strike? What would the player expect God to do?

Jesus did indeed encourage us to "ask the Father anything in my name." Is it proper now to wonder what request is out of bounds?

As in all things, we look to Jesus as the teacher. His first instruction concerns the intimacy that is required for personal prayer. Jesus said: "But whenever you pray, go into your room...and pray to your Father who is in secret....When you are praying, do not heap up empty phrases as the Gentiles do; for they think that they will be heard because of their many words. Do not be like them, for your Father knows what you need before you ask him" (Matthew 6:6–8). He then gave us the prayer that we call the Our Father.

Prayer must first include praise: "Hallowed be thy name," and then an acknowledgment that the Father is in charge. "Thy Kingdom come, thy will be done." What might be considered requests comes next. "Give us this day our daily bread," is really to declare that we depend on our Father for everything essential to life. The plea, "Forgive us our trespasses," makes the admission that we are still self-centered and have been ungrateful even unto this present moment of need. "And lead us not into temptation, but deliver us from evil" asks the wisdom to know when we are in moral danger and the strength to flee the allurement to sin.

True prayer is possible only through the Holy Spirit who alone allows us to say: "Jesus is Lord" (*cf.* 1 Corinthians 12:3). When the Father is asked to take sides between his children, we must wonder whether we are really asking in the name of Jesus. That pertains in sports or in the game of life. He is not going to give an advantage to one of his children over another, beyond the gifts that he has already given us. Our job is to do our best. That is all that our heavenly Father, or any parent, expects.

Nor should our distractions be a deterrent. Some falsely consider distractions as the incursion of mundane thoughts into the realm of the heavenly. That might be the case if we were enjoying the bliss of contemplation. But in everyday prayer we ought to begin by telling God exactly what at that moment is on our mind, both our joys and our concerns. Do not lovers share their thoughts? So we can say that what is on our mind will be of interest to God. But then, of course, he expects us to listen to what he wants us to know and to do.

We believe Jesus, who is Truth.

We often declare that we *believe* in something. We really mean that we accept something as true, valuable or beneficial strongly enough to base our actions upon this knowledge. We may arrive at this conviction from our personal experience or through a reasoning process. Yet there is really only one way that we know the truth about something that will justify the expression "I believe." This is when we accept something as true entirely on the word of someone whose integrity and experience we respect, in whom we have faith.

Thus we have faith only in persons; that is, we believe to be true all they say because their word is trustworthy. To be precise, we believe only in *people,* not things or facts or ideas. This applies in the natural order. The supernatural virtue of faith, which we have received as a gift from God, compels us to believe in Jesus, namely, to accept the truth he has brought from the heavenly Father and to live in accord with that teaching.

What God wants his people to know we find in the Holy Scriptures, including the Old Testament, but especially what we read in the Gospels and Epistles. Hence, with the grace of faith we accept the words of Jesus as the truth. Jesus gave his church the authority to teach, and so we believe in the church when she proclaims what Jesus taught us through the Apostles.

> And Jesus came and said to them, "All authority in heaven and on earth has been given to me. Go therefore and make disciples of all nations, baptizing them in the name of the Father and of the Son and of the Holy Spirit, and teaching them to

obey everything that I have commanded you. And remember, I am with you always, to the end of the age." (Matthew 28:18–20)

So, can God lie? What an outrageous thought, comparable to calling someone a deceiver, an enemy of truth. That is the very reason why those who do not agree with what the Bible says must rationalize their dissent with the platitude: "That's not what God meant." In other words, God is not a bold-faced liar. He is just ambivalent. Yet for intellectual honesty one must make a choice. Either we believe Jesus when he declares that he is the Son of God, accepting all he has said about his church, or else we must reject the Bible as God's Word (and just a human document), claiming that Jesus never said what he is reported to have said. Otherwise, we must call Jesus a liar.

Yet interpretations that cannot be equally true have been put forth from the very beginning. Most fundamentally, for example, Jesus is either the Son of God or he is not. One cannot have it both ways. The Gospels certainly declare that he proclaimed that he and the Father were one. The scribes and Pharisees understand that he was making himself equal to God. "He blasphemes!" they shouted. But if he was not God, of course he was a liar. Then the Catholic church's claim to possess the authority of God to teach is a sham.

In human affairs, a question asked out of curiosity or ignorance that goes over the line can be ignored or diverted with vague statements. However, anyone who has the right to know must be told the truth. Since we are God's people, created freely by him and loved by him, it is inconceivable that Jesus would not tell us the truth.

Our faith in Jesus, believing all he has said and living accordingly, gives us stability and removes the confusion that our own selfishness and the world's evil often bring into our life. Above all we need to keep in mind that Jesus does not merely suggest to us what we might believe and do. He tells us plainly both what we must know and how he expects us to live.

Yet faith is not enough. We need confidence in the promises of God (hope) and finally unity with God's will (love). Faith, however, is the foundation of the structure, and the strength of our trust and love depends on the firmness of our faith. So a saint instinctively understands that growth in faith will call for a deepening knowledge of Jesus. This is accomplished only through reading and listening to the Scriptures, with a special emphasis on Jesus' own words and actions. Regular reflection on the Word of God is indispensable to holiness. This practice must not be an intellectual exercise, but under the impulse of grace a search for the understanding and love of God's will in the particular circumstances of a given day. Any act of obedience means that we are saying: "I trust you, Lord and I want to love your will for me. When possible, I would also like to understand it as well."

We need now to examine more closely the prayer that Jesus taught us as the example for all our conversations with God, the attitude that applies to all personal relationships.

Our Father, who art in heaven...

The first thing that Jesus tells us is that we do not have a personal hold on God. We do not say *my* father, but *our* father, as one who is loved as a member of the family of God. A father may have a personal relationship with each of his children, but loves them as his family and not as rivals for his attention. He wants each one to be the full recipient of his love. Thus, we must not be in competition with each other, but our Father expects us to see ourselves as part of his family. He will not take sides against any of his children.

One's own personal experiences of family may cloud the relationship with our heavenly Father. Some of us have grown up without a father, because of death or desertion. Others have had disappointing experiences of family life, because of a father who was either a brute or a wimp. Only persons with those sad experiences can truly understand how their human experience affects their relationship with their Father in heaven. Yet, many have been blessed with a father who was strong, self-sacrificing and supportive in a bond of love with his wife and children. Those not so blessed have had to learn what God expects of a father from their observation of other men who are good fathers. We thank God that, even in our secular and self-absorbed society, there are so many of these around.

Indeed, our understanding of what the relationship should be with our God as Father is influenced by the experience of our earthly father, good or bad. That can be the problem. Even when our relationship with our father was good and we knew that he would do what he considered best for us, we remember that there were times we had to beg him for something, since he did not know or understand everything about us. Hence, we all need to learn to act differently with our heavenly Father.

Jesus taught us about his Father, and that he is

father to us all. Since he is a *spirit*, he is neither male nor female. We must not think that God reflects human fatherhood. Rather, we see in a human being who has fathered children a faint reflection of God's own creative power with the responsible love that is required from one who has shared in this divine attribute.

We also give the title of "Father" to priests because they reflect the fatherhood of God as the source of spiritual life and they have been called to that vocation for the purpose of nurturing the divine life given to us in baptism. For most, the influence of many priests in their life, and perhaps a particular priest during a time of special need, has been God's gift on their journey to sainthood. Even those who have suffered disappointment or even been scandalized by the conduct of a priest know well that the human reflections of our heavenly Father always fall short of his eternal goodness. Even the best of them are inadequate, and saints know that they must transcend creatures and reach to the Creator.

Our Father, as our Creator, is the source of all life. He also loved us enough to send his Son to redeem us in order that we might once more become his adopted children, sharing his divine life. This is a fundamental difference between our heavenly and earthly father. Yes, one is our eternal Father. Yet we need to remember also that our earthly father will always be our father and that means into eternity. This human relationship can never end. Every human father should take note of this connection that he has established. He links his children to the fatherhood of God and this makes Jesus, the Son of God, brother to us all.

Hallowed be thy name.

After we have acknowledged our relationship to the Father, we render homage with the phrase "hallowed be thy name," indicating that our primary intention is to praise him for his goodness. The phrase means "may your name be blessed." After all, it is the polite thing to do, since our relationship is one of creature to creator. In all things that pertain to God, we ought to remember the basic etiquette of human conversation. Would we even think of asking a friend to do us a favor immediately after our greeting?

We should understand this very well in an age when the outstretched hand is a familiar sight on a city street. If the approach is brash and the request for money is direct, we feel annoyed rather than charitable, for no one likes to have his dignity affronted by direct assault.

The same would apply to a friend or acquaintance that, at each meeting, bothers us for a favor. That is especially true if the request is right up front, without so much as a greeting, an expression of interest in one's well being, or, God forbid, a word of thanks for a favor previously asked for and received.

I wonder if God "feels" the same as we do when he is treated like that. Let us ask ourselves whether the first words in our prayer too often are similar to: "Lord, I need...I want...please help me!" Do we plead with God as a beggar would? Should not God expect to be treated as someone whom we appreciate and not just as a source for all the things we want?

It was Jesus who taught us about his Father. He told us first to greet him in accord with our relationship, just as a friend greets a friend by his name. We are first to address him as "Our Father who art in heaven," which is exactly who he is. After all, when friends meet, they first acknowledge the friendship and what it means to each of them.

Young friends hail each other with "How are things going?" Those of middle age are more apt to greet their friends with "It's good to see you." Old-timers say something akin to: "You are certainly looking good." Everyone means the same thing but from different perspectives, namely, "You are important to me. I like you."

When we greet our Father in heaven, we do the same. We tell him: "I recognize you as God, my father and creator. I thank you for everything that I have received from you." This is all summed up in the one phrase "hallowed be thy name."

Indeed, gratitude is the proper sentiment that precedes all others in our contact with a loved one, grateful that we are cherished, indeed that we are loved. It would even precede any request for forgiveness if any offense or thoughtlessness were committed since the last encounter. And it certainly must come before asking for a favor. Toward God this is even more important.

Jesus taught us what to say *before* we get down to what is really on our minds. The greeting ought not be perfunctory, but thoughtful. We certainly realize that the saints, upon turning their attention to God, used up more time than the few seconds it takes to say: "Our Father, who art in heaven, hallowed be thy name."

Like all people in love, saints eventually have little need for words, whether spoken by the lips or in the mind, like lovers who can enjoy each other's presence without saying anything. Saints learn to listen for hours to the voice of God. They prefer to hear the wisdom of God rather than their own meanderings.

Thy kingdom come.

Jesus taught us the way we are to speak with God in his response to the Apostles' plea: "Lord, teach us to pray" (Luke 11:1). Yet, how often we think that we know better. The profound simplicity of the Our Father cannot be improved upon. It must be the example for all prayer. After we have greeted our Father who is Creator with the title that proclaims our relationship and offered praise and thanks to him in one phrase ("hallowed be thy name"), we are ready to begin the "petitions." Jesus puts them in proper order, according to their importance. The next two of the remaining six will focus on the Father's glory and not on our personal needs.

Jesus has taught us that we must first acknowledge that we understand our destiny is the kingdom of heaven, not an earthly paradise. The good thief on the cross turned to Jesus and said: "Jesus, remember me when you come into your kingdom." Jesus responded: "Truly I tell you, today you will be with me in Paradise" (Luke 23:42–43). We, too, must look forward to that eternal kingdom. Yet we still live in the kingdom on earth that Jesus spoke about so often in the many comparisons that the Gospels relate: *The kingdom of heaven is like a mustard seed…is like yeast…is like a landowner…is like ten virgins, etc.* So we see that it is very much a developing kingdom that we are part of, which we must work toward making a reality "on earth as it is in heaven."

Since the kingdom of God will prevail no matter

what we might say or do, we are not really praying for its success. We are simply declaring that we want to be part of that success.

The kingdom in heaven where Jesus reigns in glory is one of justice and peace, a kingdom of love. The kingdom on earth (which is the church) is made up of those who would live in justice and peace and love, empowered by the Spirit, but so often falling short. Jesus is king and Mary is queen of heaven. But their kingdom on earth is made up of imperfect beings still struggling with sin, with their own selfish interests.

Hence, in the Lord's Prayer, when we say "thy kingdom come," we are in effect admitting this deficiency, especially in ourselves. We recognize that it is a personal responsibility, most importantly in areas where we have influence. We would renounce all hypocrisy in our dealings with others, so often the cause of dissension. We would put aside personal ambition at the expense of others, so often the cause of injustices. And we will be ready to do only what is good even to those who hate us, so that we can live in love. That is how we pray: "thy kingdom come." Because it is really just one petition, we then follow it with a phrase that links the kingdom of heaven with the kingdom of earth. It is inconceivable for a saint to separate the two places.

Thy will be done on earth as it is in heaven.

What Jesus tells us with the Our Father is that we must be absorbed into the will of the Father, as he is one with the Father. The bond of love bridges heaven and earth. As Jesus will return to the Father, so we must anticipate that same purpose even as we live out our days in this world.

Love is a terribly risky proposition. It demands trust on each side. In human relationships this trust is usually less than perfect. Our sinful nature just keeps getting in the way. As long as we do not expect the other to be perfect (that is, "just like me"), then the essence of the love will remain steadfast. It will circumvent every form of misunderstanding.

When dealing with God, the misunderstanding is always on our side. In the prayer to our heavenly Father, after expressing our intention to help bring about his kingdom here on earth, we assure him that we will continue to love him as he has asked, by living as he expects. "Thy will be done on earth as it is in heaven." What God wants will be fulfilled. After all, God does not change his mind according to circumstances. He is eternal, the "everlasting now." This is the mystery of God's unchanging, eternal nature. What our prayer declares is that we want to conform to his love for us, to do his will and not expect that he will do for us exactly what we want.

In the garden of Gethsemane, Jesus prayed "Father, if you are willing, remove this cup from me; yet, not my will but yours be done" (Luke 22:42). This certainly teaches us that in our weak and painful focus on our own situation we often may express what we would like God to do for us. That is fine as far as it goes. He is not adverse to us expressing our feelings. But we must be open to the possibility that our Father might have a different plan for us, different from what we have planned for ourselves. Otherwise, we will not be surrendering to him, but forming the kingdom according to our plan. Such surrender, of course, constitutes true love.

The extended meaning of "thy will be done" might be expressed thus: "O Father of us all, I know that you love me and so will do what is best for me. Help me to love your will as you guide me toward eternal life. Let me not waste my energies in trying to make you see it my way."

Never trust a stranger!

We do not rely on the promise of someone whom we have never met before, or even heard of. Perhaps experience has taught us that nice-looking people are not always honest. Very simply, you can only put confidence in the word of someone who, by your personal experience, has always kept his promises or whose goodness you have witnessed over a period of time. An intelligent person never trusts another until he proves worthy of it. Self-centered people are untrustworthy, as are frightened people, braggarts or those interested in exercising power.

In human relationships knowledge is the basis for trust or the lack of it. In the supernatural order, our relationship to God is based on our faith in his word, how much we really believe him; that is, what we know about him from the Scriptures or from our personal contact in prayer. Thus our trust in God can be only as strong as our knowledge of him, i.e., what we believe about him. The deeper our experience with God and the stronger our trust in his promises, the less we need to have him "prove himself."

Jesus has made this promise: "Those who eat my flesh and drink my blood have eternal life, and I will raise them up on the last day" (John 6:54). Throughout the Gospels there are other promises. For example, in

Luke 9:23–24 we read: "If any want to become my followers, let them deny themselves and take up their cross daily and follow me. For those who want to save their life will lose it, and those who lose their life for my sake will save it." This is not exactly the promise of a rose garden. We Christians live on the assurance that our faithfulness to Jesus will bring us to an eternal life of glory. We trust the word of Jesus and live accordingly.

Those who will not trust God at all live in despair, without hope. Others, on the contrary, live on promises that God never made. This is called presumption. For instance, he never promised that everyone will go to heaven. Those who reject him for a life of sin will be cast into eternal fire. That is also his promise.

There is no need for trust when we understand perfectly what God is up to in our lives. But when difficult things are happening, when our days are the darkest and we cannot understand why a loving God permits suffering, then we are called upon to trust in God, which is living the virtue of hope. Thence we are prepared to love. For you can only love someone you trust, and you can only trust someone whom you know well. Thus, the more we believe who God is, the more we trust him. And the more we trust him, the more we can love him. Then we will believe more strongly, and then trust more fearlessly, and then love more ardently and so on and so on and so on.

Lovers trust the beloved; saints trust God. They do not put him to the test by looking for favors.

Give us this day our daily bread.

Does a hungry child plead for food from a mother or father? Does a parent need to hear any more than

"Mommy, I'm hungry," to provide something to eat? Since our heavenly Father always knows when we are hungry, we really do not even have to tell him. But as a parent is pleased when a child recognizes a need that only mommy or daddy can fulfill, so too does God like to hear us say: "I'm hungry." With this trust of a child, we ask for our daily bread.

Of course food is not all we need every day. There is clothing and shelter and people to love us. There is strength in adversity and courage when difficulties block our path. There is the smile that will make us forget how hard things are. There is the grace to live as Christians in a pagan world and the perseverance to continue in the face of failure. There is the opportunity to earn a living. So when we pray in the Our Father, "Give us this day our daily bread," we are really letting God know that we trust that he will provide at this particular time what is necessary for our life and for our good. He may not come himself, nor send an angel, but he will certainly send someone. As long as we are doing our part and ready to help others wherever possible, we are sure to be fed. "Is there anyone among you who, if your child asks for a fish, will give a snake instead of a fish? Or if the child asks for an egg, will give a scorpion? If you then, who are evil, know how to give good gifts to your children, how much more will the heavenly Father give the Holy Spirit to those who ask him" (Luke 11:11–13).

As a matter of practical preparation for prayer, we need in the evening hours to reflect on the difficulties and challenges we faced during that day. In the morning we might project our thoughts toward the responsibilities we will be called to fulfill in the hours ahead.

A prayer for guidance at midday will help us notice the deficiencies of our morning efforts and project us toward greater purity of intention in our work for the remainder of the day.

In whatever form we pray the sentiments expressed in the petition of the Our Father, "Give us this day our daily bread," we can be assured that God always gives us what we might need, although not always what we are looking for. But if we *trust* our Father, we always get an increase in the gifts of the Holy Spirit. These gifts are not obtained by human efforts. They are truly gifts: *wisdom* and *understanding* to love his will; *knowledge* and *fortitude* to follow it bravely; *counsel* and *piety* to fulfill it with love; and finally *fear of the Lord* to find true peace in God's will. For all this we have the guarantee of Jesus himself, and our future efforts will contribute to the success of our role in advancing the kingdom.

Forgive us our trespasses as we forgive...

Now we come to the heart of our prayer and the essence of our relationship to the Father. We are among the sinners who were redeemed by his Son who became man. He suffered and died to free us from sin, to make it possible for us to become children of God. For this each of us must be eternally grateful. We need also to be eternally vigilant since we still are capable of sin, on the verge of betraying our Father's goodness. Hence, this relationship of sinner to a merciful Father must never be far from our mind. It necessarily affects every aspect of our relationship to our Father in heaven and to his Son and the Holy Spirit. We read that the saints, as they were drawn closer into the life of the Triune God, became more conscious of their own unworthiness to be loved by God and to receive his favors.

To grow in holiness, we need more and more to show our gratitude for the Father's mercy and the suffering of Jesus by our willingness to forgive those who offend us. Hence, we do not hesitate to put the condition on our request for mercy when we add in the Lord's Prayer: "as we forgive those who trespass against us." But that is the difficulty. We say it, but we often hope that God does not take us seriously. To forgive promptly is heroic charity.

To err is human; to forgive divine. Thus do human beings acknowledge two realities; namely, how easy it is to make mistakes and excuse ourselves for our failures, and yet how difficult it is to accept the admitted wrongdoing of another when we have suffered from that malice.

To forgive and love even more afterward is something only God can do, or one to whom he gives that special grace. Such a grace requires the humility to admit our sinfulness and ask God for mercy. In the Gospels Jesus says that the Father expects us to be forgiving toward our fellow sinners before he can forgive us. Justice calls for mutual forgiveness, namely, that we harbor no anger toward another who may have injured us. We must go out of our way to forgive. "For if you forgive others their trespasses, your heavenly Father will also forgive you; but if you do not forgive others, neither will your Father forgive your trespasses" (Matthew 6:14–15).

"I will never forgive him as long as I live," the wronged party might say as the immediate response to a grievous evil done him. If it is meant, of course, it is the pathway to eternal perdition. It excludes one from God's forgiveness, which all of us need for salvation. As time goes on, a good Christian may reach the dilemma: "I want to forgive him, but I can't find it in myself to do so." And this they will say at the same time that they remember the words of Jesus: "If you do not forgive, you will not be forgiven." Yet that same Christian will pray daily: "Forgive us our trespasses as we forgive those who trespass against us."

But it is proper to ask: "Can even God really forgive someone who does not ask to be forgiven?" The answer is: "No, he cannot." Otherwise hell would not exist. Yet the Scripture is clear: "Then he will say to those at his left hand, 'You that are accursed, *depart from me into the eternal fire prepared for the devil and his angels*'" (Matthew 25:41, emphasis added).

To forgive is divine. God's nature is love, and love always looks to forgive. So we get every opportunity to say that we love him. Indeed, he is patient and coaxes us in so many ways to say that we are sorry. He offers us grace to strengthen us against sinning again. Yet there must be a response on our part to say humbly: "Be merciful to me, O Lord! I am a sinner." Then he gladly embraces us and forgives all.

So what do saints do with someone who seeks to do them wrong? First, they remind themselves of their own sinfulness, so there will be never any desire for revenge but instead a readiness to forgive when the other asks. Every opportunity is offered, with great kindness, to make it easy for the other to seek forgiveness. This allows the freedom that love requires. Even God cannot force us to love him, since he too needs our free expression of sorrow in response to his grace freely given.

And lead us not into temptation, but...
This petition of the Our Father says that we do not expect a life free of temptations. Indeed, we may have heard the maxim: if you wish to become a *great* saint, you must expect *great* temptations. Yet we certainly do not want to be surprised, so we pray that we will always recognize the face of temptation when it emerges. Unfortunately, too often we might find ourselves overwhelmed before we even recognize that we are being drawn toward sin. God certainly does not lead us *into* temptation, although he may allow us to learn from our foolishness. We must ask his grace *to lead us away* from temptation. This grace is the wisdom to anticipate temptations and the strength to turn away.

Sin is attractive. We are always susceptible to gluttony and to lust, to revenge and to laziness, to rash judgment and to violence, to dishonesty and to many subtle forms of pride. "Discipline yourselves, keep alert. Like a roaring lion your adversary the devil prowls around, looking for someone to devour" (1 Peter 5:8).

"The devil made me do it." That line from the routine of a popular comedian from time past has too often been put forth in a more familiar refrain: "I couldn't help myself." Both statements, of course, imply that somehow the very nature of humanity is corrupt. We know that, as a result of original sin, we are indeed prone to selfishness. That admission, at least, makes us redeemable. But to say that we are inherently wicked is to surrender, and not because we don't want to fight but because we feel that victory is impossible.

Which leads to a question: If you did meet a lion, ravenous with hunger or defensive of its territory, which would you do? Challenge it to combat, or put a lot of distance between the animal and yourself as fast as possible? The prudent answer is obvious. Then why do we speak about "fighting" temptation, or "struggling" with addictions? Such fighting or struggling aggravates the emotions. This could be a subtle temptation to engage in the combat, because it would seem like virtue to oppose evil. But often it allows for some physical or intellectual excitement, with a consequent forbidden feeling of power without the guilt, because we say to ourselves: "I'm trying my best."

There is really only one defense against temptation; namely, learn from past experiences to recognize it quickly and then run and run and run even faster. In practice that means either to become removed from the actual situation (persons, places or things) that excites the attraction to sin, or distract ourselves as best we can. Then we need to put our attention toward something else. Since the mind cannot simply be emptied out, it must be trained in discipline to turn to new avenues of interest, either something very mundane or, still better, constructive and inspiring.

As we end the prayer that Jesus taught us, we seek the grace to recognize temptation, not to be fooled by Satan, the father of lies. We wish to be delivered from evil.

Loving God is not a gamble.

"Let's take a chance on love," says the old song from days past, and the refrain is all I remember. This sentiment reflects the human situation under the best of conditions. Love between human beings contains a gamble, since our ability to know the *real* person is limited. Hence we often put our trust in someone with our fingers crossed. Nevertheless, God has made us to love, an essential ingredient of our nature, so we take the chance, prudently minimizing the risks. Surprisingly, lots of time we win. With God, however, there are no risks.

We need not fear that God will betray us. Our love for God takes courage since it is not easily acquired. We still have to trust him, based on a faith that must accept him exactly as he has revealed himself in the Scriptures. As in human affairs, where we need to resist the impulse to make over the beloved in our own image, so too we must grow in knowing God as he truly is and not as we might like him to be. When our understanding is blurred and events are uncomfortable, when trust is difficult, we often try to imagine that God wants something other than our complete surrender to his will. The temptation is subtle.

To stay focused on our goal of holiness, to grow in faithfulness to the Father, our Creator, and to deepen true knowledge of Jesus, Son of God and our Redeemer, our daily prayer must be one of gratitude for his past goodness. Then we will learn to rejoice even when the will of God is obscure. We will expect that, sooner or later, the good will be apparent.

"And now faith, hope, and love abide, these three; and the greatest of these is love" (1 Corinthians 13:13). Love is the greatest because it is meant to last forever. It is a contradiction to say: "I will love you for five years. After that, adios!" Sadly, some will misuse the word when they promise: "I will love you as long as things work out." In such case it is a business relationship, not a love bond.

Yet we are fully aware that our love for God in this world, as well as any human love, is not made perfect by one act nor is completed in one moment of ecstasy. It becomes a process by which we burn out selfishness and any inclinations toward selfishness, little by little. It must be fed as a fire is fed, so it will not die out. The fuel of love is sacrifice. Hence, love for God is truly complete only when we have attained eternal glory. In heaven there is no need for faith or trust, since the promise has been fulfilled and we are in the full possession of the Beloved. On earth, meanwhile, we keep in touch with the prayer that Jesus himself taught us.

CHAPTER FOUR

a divine conspiracy

Who do people say that the Son of Man is?
—Matthew 16:13

Wise people do not pursue happiness, for they know that it is not a goal in itself, but the result of a good life. For the worldly minded, happiness becomes the end-all of existence. "As long as you don't hurt anyone, do what makes you happy," friends will say to friends as a gesture of compassion. Or the desperate individual may find comfort with the justification: "After all, don't I deserve a little happiness?"

We know, of course, that Jesus said the contrary: "Blessed [happy] are you when people revile you and persecute you...your reward is great in heaven" (Matthew 5:11–12). Saints discover happiness where Jesus told us that we would find it. Those who concern themselves with enjoyment as a first principle do not become saints. Human wisdom focuses on the present world and fails to take into account our eternal destiny. Those who seek holiness pay attention to the Jesus who draws us to himself in a way that is deemed foolish by the worldly wise.

Unfortunately, it is possible that some who would be holy think that we should ignore real life. They want to keep their eyes always cast upward, to enjoy the idea of being in love with God. Such spiritual laziness contradicts the very idea of being holy. Saints never forget that love implies responsibilities.

To surrender our self-interest without reservation to the will of the one whom we love does not come easy to us sinners. Indeed, this will be impossible without first acquiring a very intimate knowledge of the Son of God, who became man and who leads us to the Father. Then we will understand the full impact of his words and example for our lives. Jesus and his Father are one, and only the Son knows the Father and he to whom the Son has decided to reveal him. He left this world so that he might send us the Holy Spirit, who draws us into the divine union of persons as well as into union with all others who strive to be one with God.

To draw close to Jesus calls for a steadily deepening knowledge of his person and what he taught when he lived among us. Knowledge, after all, is the first step in learning to love, because we can only trust one whom we know well. Without trust, love is not possible. The deeper the knowledge, the stronger the trust; the stronger the trust, the more intimate the love.

So the desire to attain holiness, which is love of God, demands a deep knowledge and understanding of Jesus himself. We must seek this knowledge of the *real* Jesus through our reflective reading of the Gospels. Otherwise we are in danger of creating a Jesus according to our own image.

Mother knows best.

To have the desire to be holy, to be good, is an abstraction unless it focuses on something or someone very real. Since holiness, simply put, is conforming oneself to God's will, the love must be directed toward the person who brings us into the divine life, the Son made man. To get close to Jesus, we are no better served than to be close to the one who is closest to him, his mother. After all, who knows a son better than the mother? The father is also important here, especially since this couple is most unique. To understand the relationship of Jesus to his parents is the first step in understanding Jesus himself. A reflection on the special circumstances of his birth and early life is the place to begin.

Simply because he was chosen by this wonderful woman, Mary, to be her husband, we know that Joseph must have been an exceptional man. When Mary gave her answer to the angel who announced God's plan for her, "Let it be done with me according to your word," Joseph's life also turned in a totally unexpected direction (Luke 1:38). We might say that for a while his life came to a complete stop. The beautiful and wonderful woman he had married (although they had not yet begun to live together) was pregnant, and not by him. I can only imagine that Mary told Joseph the full story the first chance she got and explained its mystery in the best way she was able.

Being a *just* man, he would not humiliate her, but in accord with the Law of Moses that called for a divorce if a woman got pregnant before moving in with her husband, he would do so without a public display.

How long his confusion lasted we do not know, but eventually an angel in a dream gave him the direction he needed. She was, after all, everything that his heart had found so wonderful when he had proposed marriage. The joy he felt when she had accepted him would continue, although nothing could ever be routine. We know that their lives would take even more unpredictable turns.

Twelve years later, after finding Jesus in the temple, Mary was still "pondering these things in her heart." She and Joseph believed that her son was God's Son and also the Messiah who was promised to Abraham. Yet from the very beginning there were difficulties. They faced together the need to travel to Bethlehem just as her time was getting near, followed by the birth in a stable without the amenities of the house in Nazareth. Soon followed the command to take the child and his mother into Egypt. Mary found comfort in having the faithful Joseph at her side. In all this we want to understand the Son, who would allow his mother and father to go through such hard times. We marvel at the mystery of God's will.

We still do not fathom the exact meaning of Mary's question of the angel: "How can this be, since I am a virgin?" (Luke 1:34). Did she just mean at this time? Or had she and Joseph agreed, as many think, to a virginal marriage, at least for a time? But we certainly know that her answer to the angel included an understanding that she would henceforth remain a virgin. Joseph's love for this fantastic woman, whom the Holy Spirit too had chosen to be his spouse, would become more profound and wonderful and exhilarating.

In a painting of the Nativity scene, one artist has

captured their love. He focuses our admiration, not on the mother and child, but on strong, silent Joseph who is gazing with affection on his wife as she nurses God's Son. This couple can teach us about Jesus, since they watched him grow from infancy to young adulthood.

Mary's first love

Before we move on, let us add a further reflection about the man who was closest to Jesus and Mary and the model for every Christian. He was chosen to be responsible for the care of the Son of God and his mother. He remained side by side with Mary from the birth of Jesus in Bethlehem until he had grown. We only know for certain that Joseph died sometime between the finding in the temple and the marriage feast at Cana. Joseph's task was done when Jesus was able to support his mother and the two of them could proceed by divine plan on their joint mission to bring about our redemption.

Because Joseph died in the presence of Jesus and Mary, we invoke him as the patron of a happy death. Joseph is also honored as the Patron of the Universal Church, since his wife is the mother of the church, the Body of Christ. Together they cared for Jesus until his maturity, with Joseph as protector and provider for the Holy Family. Also he was the young virgin's first love. Who better than Joseph can we choose to be companion and guide on our journey to holiness?

Mary loved Joseph and accepted him in marriage before she knew of her predestined role as the mother of God. I cannot accept the idea that she fell in love other than with a vibrant young man of twenty or so. She is thought to have been about sixteen. When

Joseph accepted his role as a virginal husband and he reflected on the wonderful woman he married, his willing sacrifice for her intensified his love and set him on the road to sanctity. His journey was in the company of Jesus and Mary, not unlike our own must be.

For meditation, I offer you my favorite picture of the Holy Family, which expresses their relationship as father and mother to child. They are back in Nazareth, and Joseph stands in the foreground with a six-month-old Jesus in his arms. He is looking on the child with tenderness. Mary is in the background, not cooking or cleaning, but sound asleep on a cot.

We can say up front that Joseph must have been quite a man to be chosen by this most fantastic woman as her husband. With this in mind, have not young women in every age prayed to Joseph to lead them to the man of their dreams? In addition he is the inspiration for husbands to love their wives and children faithfully and selflessly as gifts from God. Those with a special call to serve the church as the presence of Jesus in this world, namely, priests and religious, easily see Joseph as the model of faithful service for the glory of God. His acceptance of God's will under difficult circumstances is everyone's inspiration to trust in the love of the Father for *all* his children in the midst of often confusing challenges.

Whatever our vocation in life by God's will, we are called to become saints in accordance with gospel values, epitomized by a life that is poor in spirit, chaste and in full obedience to God's will in every circumstance. None of us can look for a better model than Joseph.

You can't be serious!

The church refers to Jesus and Mary and Joseph as the Holy Family and presents them as the model for all Christian families. This needs some looking into.

Catholics, in general, have no difficulty looking to Mary and Joseph as models for their individual lives as holy people. But the reaction of many to the idea of Mary and Joseph (and Jesus) as examples of family life is one of skepticism. Mary and Joseph, as a married couple, as a father and mother, do not reflect the image most of us know from our growing up. To illustrate, I pass on a story told to me many years ago.

The woman at Mass was trying to keep her three little ones under control. They looked to be about two, four and six years old. Her husband appeared totally unconcerned as he concentrated on the homily. The priest must have noticed her difficulty. At the door of the church after Mass, he suggested to the young mother that she look to Mary, mother of the Holy Family, for guidance in caring for her children. Her frazzled response said it all: "What does she know, with only one! And my husband is no Joseph."

This woman is not alone in finding Jesus, Mary and Joseph hard to accept as a practical example for the Christian family. The mother was without sin, the child was the Son of God, and Joseph had graciously and lovingly accepted a virginal relationship with Mary, his wife. Although full of the usual sacrifices needed to take care of a household and earn a living, the family life of Mary and Joseph certainly cannot be considered the norm. So how do we speak of the Holy Family as our model and thereby have a better and deeper understanding of the Son?

In the first place, the example is not one of pragmatism, a how-to model. The circumstances of the first family of Nazareth go beyond that. Rather, from them we learn about the essence of family relationships. They reflect the perfect example of the Christian life itself, which is fundamentally one of relationships, beginning with the relationship within God himself, the Blessed Trinity. Who is this woman, the mother? Who is this man, the father? Who is this child? How do they relate to each other?

All three are needed to make up a family: the father, the mother and the child. The family begins to exist precisely when the relationship of each to the others begins, which is simultaneous. The father is not a father a moment before the mother is a mother, and that precisely when the child comes into being. This becomes an eternal relationship. It lasts forever.

Parents may in death cease to be husband and wife, but they never cease to be father and mother to a particular child. This eternal family relationship between human beings is a sublime reflection of the life of God, who are three persons related from and for eternity. In a family relationship each person is a distinct human being, each with a different function and nature, but they constitute *one* family. In the Trinity of distinct Divine Persons, there is only *one* nature. God is one and so we truthfully say "God is love," a union of persons.

So in this context we look to Mary and Joseph and see how they related to each other and then together and singly to Jesus. From them we learn how we must relate to each other, since we all have this special relationship to Jesus, Son of God.

In every human family the child is the one who makes it a family, and the welfare of the child (or children) will steer the family's decisions (as in the flight into Egypt). Parents are designated by God to raise the child according to his divine plan, and their guidance should not reflect their own ambitions. "For I have come down from heaven, not to do my own will, but the will of him who sent me" (John 6:38). Parents are responsible before God, and the child obeys the parents until adulthood. "Then he went down with them and came to Nazareth, and was obedient to them. His mother treasured all these things in her heart" (Luke 2:51).

Mary and Joseph were in love, since each had chosen the other before they knew of God's plan for them. Once married and responsible for a child, their love is focused through the child, is bonded in the child. Everything about the child is of mutual concern. Just so, all husbands and wives grow in love through their roles as mother and father of the children they have begotten in God.

The most striking insight we have of the family life of Nazareth is the obedience that Jesus gives to Mary and Joseph and his acceptance of their dedicated love for him as they fulfilled God's will. From this example of Jesus, we understand that obedience is the first step on the journey toward the goal of perfect charity.

With Jesus and Mary

We may be able to separate Jesus from Joseph in some respects, but we cannot separate Jesus from his mother. From the cross, he gave Mary to us as our mother also. Thus we can attain holiness only with and through Mary and with the example of Mary's love for Jesus. Their unity began at the very beginning, when she accepted her role as mother of the Redeemer. After that they are inseparable, first in the physical sense but also in purpose during the life of Jesus. After the Ascension of Jesus into heaven, she remained with the Apostles as the mother of the church.

Her first lesson to us was given after she learned from the angel Gabriel that her kinswoman Elizabeth, until now barren, was with child in her old age and was already in her sixth month. Mary immediately rose up and went into the hill country of Judea to the house of Zachary. Of course, Jesus was with her.

Visitors to your home can make life interesting and often exciting. Even for family or friends, however, three months could be overdoing it. Yet there might be a reason that would make a visit of three months a welcome gift. Try pregnancy. Mary knew that her elderly cousin would have difficulty getting around. Zachary, the husband, was probably getting desperate. Mary arrived after a long trip from Nazareth, concerned only for the person who needed her.

Since she could not phone ahead to alert them, I truly believe that Mary sent a messenger before her. After all, that is the polite thing to do, and above all the mother of God would be courteous. Under any circumstances, Zachary and Elizabeth would have been glad to see her. Now they were overjoyed, her help was most welcome and so Mary stayed on until the birth of John the Baptist.

Elizabeth also knew that Mary was pregnant, for she was aware that the child in her womb "leaped for joy" when her cousin from Nazareth greeted her (Luke 1:41). "And why has this happened to me, that the mother of my Lord comes to me?" (Luke 1:43). So these women, both carrying their first child, were together for three months. Even acknowledging the uniqueness of each pregnancy, we reflect on the two women sharing special secrets. Their conversations can only be imagined, and no doubt only by mothers who can remember when they awaited the arrival of their firstborn.

With Mary as our model, we need to remember that as Christians we "carry" Jesus with us wherever we go. We must be ready to go wherever and to whomever we know that he wants us to take him. This will certainly influence our conversations. Each time should be a spiritual experience, with a desire to bring joy or at least relief, provided that we are welcome. We must want to be instruments of peace.

We must also know how long (minutes or hours) is long enough, and then leave when our continued presence would interfere with God's grace. Remember that Mary left when her work of charity was done. She would not want to wear out her welcome. Saints know that God is not obliged to any of us and that no one is indispensable. Our humility should allow another to be God's instrument when circumstances change. Mary, who loves all her children, will then do the best for each one.

"Here is your mother" (John 19:27).
We probably will not reach the heights of holiness at any time during our lives. We might in our last days. In the meantime we must work at it. Saints never

retire. The blessed mother of Jesus had not concluded her work when Jesus ascended into heaven. The purpose of her life was still not complete.

We can imagine that Mary felt some temporary loneliness after her Son left this world to send the Holy Spirit. Women of faith, even the Immaculate Virgin, can miss a loved one. Mary had lost her husband and now Jesus. But we know that she did not return to Nazareth immediately in order to mourn her loss. She stayed with the Apostles and other disciples in Jerusalem to await the coming of the Paraclete. She had to bring forth his Body, the church, as she had conceived and brought forth her only begotten Son by the power of the Holy Spirit. "When they [the Apostles] had entered the city, they went to the room upstairs where they were staying....All these were constantly devoting themselves to prayer, together with certain women, including Mary the mother of Jesus, as well as his brothers" (Acts 1:13–14).

Mary lived, according to an ancient tradition, to be seventy-two years of age. Since she was nearly fifty years old when Jesus died, her "retirement" lasted over twenty years. By the way, have you thought about our Blessed Lady having gray hair?

We might wish that we knew more about those twenty years. But we can certainly accept that Mary did not sit around without a task to do. Rather, it is more likely that she continued to be a valuable member of her Nazareth community and later at Ephesus with Saint John. No doubt she received the disciples of Jesus on visits to her home, and she must have joined the early Christian communities that gathered for the "breaking of the bread" and on special occasions. With the same faith as ours, she received her Son in Holy Communion. I personally like to think of her having heart-to-heart chats with Peter and John.

Indeed, she may have been "retired" because her work as mother of Jesus was finished. But her life did not end, for she was and is the mother of the church. She was probably busier than ever and never got the chance to get that empty feeling.

All widows and widowers, who are "lost" because their main work in life is over or they have moved away from family and friends, may want to look back. Their holiness, however, will depend on accepting the challenge of the future. It may be acceptable for saints to make an occasional visit to the past, but they must focus on the present. They know that the future will take care of itself. Mary, wife of Joseph and mother of Jesus, is the model. No self-pity. She was a good neighbor and friend who found interest in others. She even did "church" work.

Mothers are always mothers.

They want to feed us, to comfort us, to correct us, to warn us. For an earthly mother it continues until her death. For our heavenly mother it continues until *our* death. No man can resist a request from his earthly mother, even when it goes against his practical judgment. Should we not believe that Jesus also responds to Mary's concern for us? Do we not call her mother, too? He has even sent her to visit us on earth.

Mary has been an intimate part of the life of the church as a whole and nations in particular throughout the centuries. The saints have shown us that she was always close to them. All this leaves no doubt that

Our Lady is inseparable from the holiness of the church and the interior life of individuals. To make steady progress in our journey toward sanctity, it behooves each one to make sure that Mary as mother has a special place in our relationship to her Son, to guide us in the service of the church and to strengthen us in the faithful fulfillment of our responsibilities.

The sophistication of later years never destroys the simplicity of the relationship we have to our earthly mothers. We feel like a child in her presence, and she often treats us that way. So, too, we need the confidence of a child when we think of Mary as our mother, keeping before our mind's eye the picture of the young mother of Nazareth. Our conversation with her must be that childlike. She will then lead us to holiness.

Pictures of the Madonna, mother and child, are among the favorite expressions of Christian art. Our reflections on the new mother with her child bring us to the amazing awareness that our future is reflected there, in somewhat the same way we feel when we look at our own parents' wedding picture. Mary, the mother of the Redeemer, is the second Eve, the mother of all those who are the children of God. She is the mother of the church.

As a mother prepares her child for a successful future and is ever conscious of that responsibility, so too does Mary help all her children fulfill the divine will, which is nothing less than union with the Trinity of Divine Persons through her Son. In short, her responsibility is to bring us to holiness of life. She links us to all past generations of her children and to those who are still to be born. Hence, she cannot grow old.

We have all seen the promise of eternal love, which is God's life, reflected from the faces of young people who have just married. We have seen it even more so when a young mother nestles a new baby in her lap. Such a scene is a look into the future. Does not a woman, when her first grandchild is born, look back and then ahead? Is not her vision a projection of God's life, from and into eternity? Is she not a link in the chain of human creation that reaches back to Eve, "the mother of all living?" (Genesis 3:20).

Which picture of your mother do you favor? Is it the one taken on her wedding day or the one with her at your wedding? Maybe it is the one taken on her (their) fiftieth wedding anniversary, surrounded by her children and grandchildren? A man once showed me such pictures. Actually his favorite was of himself at six months of age in his mother's arms, because he was in it and his mother was so young.

Yes, old mothers remind us of the end of life. That is why the Blessed Mother is always young, because she projects the future. Did she not appear to Bernadette at Lourdes and the children at Fatima as their very young mother? In the *Pieta,* Michelangelo's masterpiece, she appears younger than Jesus, whose dead body she cradles on her lap. When Mary was assumed into heaven body and soul, she was seventy-two years old and had nurtured the young church for twenty years after Pentecost. Yet, few artists have painted her as elderly.

We do not become saints apart from the mother of Jesus. She is queen of heaven and earth. She is the queen of angels and saints. Without our submission to her care, sanctity will be beyond our reach.

Why don't we do it "my way"?

Not long after we set out on the journey to holiness, we all learned to expect obstacles along the way. This happened because we made great plans to do wonderful things for God, and they did not always work out. It does seem that God wants it that way.

Whenever any of our well-laid plans are disrupted, we might do well to remember that God once made life difficult for his favorite people. When Mary and Joseph were preparing happily for the birth of Jesus in Nazareth, in their simple yet comfortable home, "…a decree went out from Emperor Augustus that all the world should be registered….Joseph also went from the town of Nazareth in Galilee to Judea, to the city of David called Bethlehem…" (Luke 2:1, 4). So, in her ninth month and on mule back, Mary made that arduous trip with Joseph. While at Bethlehem, in a crowded hostel, Jesus was ready to be born. So, for the sake of privacy, Joseph took Mary to the stable, and Mary gave birth apart from friends and in the company of animals. The King of Kings lacked the most basic attentions of the ordinary peasant. No one would know about this great happening except, by God's design, the simple and unimportant shepherds.

As Mary pondered all these events, she might have questioned: "But, Lord, this is your Son. I would expect that you could have arranged things better for him?" To further exasperate the situation, they were soon fleeing into Egypt for a long stay.

Mary and Joseph trusted that they would eventually understand God's reasoning. We do now. The Father wanted his Son to arrive with no pretense of glory and not heralded by the great ones of this world.

He became one of us in a way that would preclude any hint of frightening power. So too, we will always know that Mary our mother understands the human frustration at plans gone awry, even after we have planned well.

Many parents can empathize with the family who had prepared for two carefree weeks on a mountain lake with their three youngsters. After one hour on the road and four more to go, the fan belt breaks. There are several hours waiting in a service station before the trip resumes. With just one hour short of journey's end, a torrential rain makes the dirt roads impassable and the car uncomfortable. Endless hours later the journey continues. When the cottage is reached in the early morning, mother offers a prayer of thanks for the "safe" arrival. No one would fault her for adding a "rider." "Why, O Lord? We planned well. The rest was up to you." The remainder of the vacation went superbly. And for many summers thereafter they could reminisce and enjoy a good laugh. *Remember the year the car broke down not long after we left the house?*

I often wonder if in later years Joseph ever said to Mary something like: "Honey, do you remember the night that Jesus was born?"

Alert for warning signs

Holiness is not just being close to God and enjoying his presence. It means to accept his will, especially when that will is often so difficult to understand because our desires and expectations can often be so different. On our journey we certainly need the grace to persevere, yet always being suspicious that our

human understanding of what is best can be mis-
guided. We need to be on the lookout for indications of
God's way, and such readiness demands faith and
trust, the same virtues Mary and Joseph practiced as
parents of God's Son.

We see this when Jesus was twelve years old. He
had gone with his parents to celebrate the Passover in
Jerusalem and remained behind when Mary and
Joseph left for home. His parents could not find him
and thought that he was lost. Jesus knew otherwise.
For he said to them, when they found him in the temple among the scholars, "Why were you searching for
me? Did you not know that I must be in my Father's
house?" (Luke 2:49).

Jesus was approaching the age for *bar mitzvah,*
when a boy takes on the responsibilities of the Jewish
faith. It was time for Jesus to declare his mission in
life. Where else would that be done but, appropriately
enough, in the temple, where God resides among his
people? He was sent to be their Messiah, as had been
promised by his Father. This was a dramatic way of
reminding Mary and Joseph that their responsibility
was to support him toward that end. But he was no
rebel. The Scripture goes on to say: "Then he went
down with them and came to Nazareth, and was obedient to them" (Luke 2:51).

We see that parents do not decide the future of
their children. But they do have the responsibility of
reading the usual signs, namely the child's capacities
and interests, and then training them with support
and guidance toward an independent choice. If the
parents show that God's will means everything to
them, the child, too, will make God a very important

part of the formula which will determine a future occupation or profession.

This, indeed, is the way parents themselves become saints, not apart from that role, but maintaining faith in God and trust in his will for their children. Each of us now follows the path we are convinced is God's will for us, even if we realize that we may have made a selfish choice in the past. Our effort to correct the course is in itself the cross that brings us toward our goal of sainthood.

Those who are parents have daily opportunities to grow in holiness. The vocation of most of God's children is marriage, and the parents' first task is to prepare their young people to become good husbands or wives, fathers or mothers. If God has other or additional plans for them, he will make that known in appropriate ways. Even so, nothing would be lost because the training needed for marriage and parenthood will serve well as preparation toward any state of life. A parent's worst mistake would be to stand in God's way. They need to remember the frequent dilemmas that Mary and Joseph faced, trying to understand the mission of God's Son. In every sense, each child is a mystery.

The relation of Mary and Joseph to Jesus remains the example for all parents in their bond of love with each other and their children. Yet there is one big difference. Mary, unlike other mothers, would become an essential part of Jesus' life and work. She would know intimately the heartache a child can bring. She always knew that it was coming. We are told that, after the finding in the temple, "his mother treasured all these things in her heart" (Luke 2:51). She certainly remembered the words of Simeon at the presentation: "And a sword will pierce your own soul too" (Luke 2:35). As the sorrowful mother, she would be called upon to offer him on the altar of the cross.

Source of our joy

Jesus, God made man, brings us the joy of anticipation, because he completes our nature that is made to the image of God, who is love. This image in us had been tarnished by original sin, although we are created to love and to be loved. Having been redeemed by the death of Jesus, we can love and be loved again. Nonetheless, our sin-scarred nature can still experience the pain of separation from God. Christian joy is lost when our beloved is no longer close at hand.

Joy is the steady companion of one who lives in God. We realize that now our union with Jesus is mystical, and we will fully experience his presence only in heaven, where we will know him as he is. The thought of that blessed encounter brings overwhelming joy. Indeed, the anticipation itself provides us strength as well. We can understand that to deprive someone of the joy of anticipation, even on a human level, would be an injustice. God does not deny us this gift.

Consider this scenario. A man lives across the country, but once a year his business brings him near his hometown. He knows about it for at least two months before, but never lets his mother know ahead of time that he will be home for a visit. He just appears on her doorstep. His excuse is that he enjoys seeing her gleeful surprise and happy face. He never thinks that he had deprived her of two months of joyful anticipation and the pleasure of getting ready for the visit. God is not that way. He wants us to enjoy preparing for his coming.

If we find that we can be easily disturbed by disappointment or discouragement, pain or loneliness, fatigue or failure, then we have forgotten for whom and for what we are waiting during our life on earth. Anticipation of what we have been promised is the basis for the joy of the saints, and our waiting often joins us to the very redemptive love that was the life of Jesus here on earth.

We all understand separation from a loved one and the joyful anticipation of a reunion. To have lost someone we love through death does create a terrible sorrow. Christians maintain that joy even in sorrow, because we believe that we will be united once again in heaven. As we all have experienced the joy in waiting for a loved one who has lived far from us for a long period of time, our faith easily transfers that joy into the anticipation of eternal life.

From the Old Testament we understand that God will eventually fulfill his every promise. To the Jews of old the promise of God that he would send a Messiah to deliver them from bondage gave hope. They lived by that promise. But they did not know when. Waiting for the coming of the Messiah, always in the far future, made them weary. They forgot the promise and lost hope. We can all appreciate the difficulty of a long wait. We might at times have even suffered a degree of anxiety.

Saints, however, are patient. They understand that God may even add a surprise when he finally fulfills his promise. The Jews never expected that the Messiah to come would be God's own Son.

The expectation that each day may bring an expression of God's love for us will make any particular moment a time of joy. Indeed, the first thought in the morning might be to wonder whether we have reached the day of our death. If such a thought would generate fear, we might question whether we have the proper foundation for Christian joy.

Indeed, we cannot live with any certainty that Jesus will have his personal encounter with us on a definite day, week, month or even year. But the responsibilities and difficulties of life must not make his delay a cause for desperation. Every day should be a day of joy, never a frustration but a realization in prayer that every day is a celebration of God's promise, amply fulfilled. With a joyful heart Mary awaited her time to give birth to the Son of God, never quite understanding what the overall plan was. So each day must begin with joy for us, too, or we are not truly serious about holiness.

The measure of holiness

Much of our waiting is burdensome. There is little cause for joy waiting in line at supermarkets, at banks or in the doctor's office. Recovering from sickness or surgery may provide only the joy of knowing that each day will be better than the last. But waiting for a loved one to come home is never difficult. Perhaps, when the one coming home is myself, I might feel a bit impatient. Eager for heaven, saints might pray: "O Lord, how much longer?" Does not Saint Paul say: "I am hard pressed between the two: my desire is to depart and be with Christ, for that is far better; but to remain in the flesh is more necessary for you" (Philippians 1:23–24).

Waiting to die when one is in no danger of dying does not count for much. Waiting to die when one knows that one's end is imminent is another story. Some wonder how they will feel when they are sure that their time is very short. The unknown frightens the human spirit. Yet many a priest in his ministry to the dying has seen some very happy people whose death is within days or hours. Priests assure those who are afraid of death that the grace of a happy death comes when it is needed, not years before. But the grace always comes.

A priest once told me of a very sick man, a husband and father and grandfather, whose family surrounded his bedside. It was December 21. He smiled at them and predicted: "It looks as if I will be home for Christmas." They knew what he meant by "going home." He did not mean his little home on Elm Street, where he and his wife had lived happily since their children had left the nest. She had died the year before, and he knew that she awaited him.

Joy envelops those who become aware that something wonderful is about to happen, and the joy is great if it is something for which they have been waiting a long time. There is great happiness and peace when the moment has arrived. Nor should it be confused with the sense of relief because the person who waits has been bored.

A saint is always ready for the coming of Jesus, anxious to meet him face to face. However, we cannot just sit around being holy. We must keep ourselves busy at fulfilling whatever it is that God expects us to do today. Saints are concerned more with getting ready than being ready. Our human nature compels us to live as long as we can, knowing that we will die when we cannot help it. Or putting it another way, we might say that a true martyr does not die for Jesus, but lives for him. We must not appear before the judgment seat of God with the job half done.

The time remaining to us must be used to our advantage. Our every action must bring to our daily lives the fruits of the death of Jesus, looking to him for mercy, justice and peace. We are strengthened by the promise of the Resurrection. Although the fullness of peace may never be attained by the world at large, it can be realized in the individual soul.

A constant joyful spirit, which anticipates the wonder of a promise fulfilled, is not something we can keep to ourselves. Others will recognize it as mark of holiness. We want to share it with others and maybe even to confound them.

CHAPTER FIVE

betrayal

God, be merciful to me, a sinner.
—Luke 18:13

I n the parable of the Pharisee and the tax collector, Jesus makes it very clear that good works alone do not put one in the good graces of God. Rather, we are justified by the acknowledgment of our constant dependency on the mercy of our heavenly Father. We need the humility to be grateful for the divine pardon received for sins committed and forgiven. And do we really know how often we were protected from occasions of sin that we foolishly almost walked into?

Being close to Jesus over a period of time does not guarantee that one will remain loyal when the challenges to our security or happiness make us fearful. We only have to think about the original twelve whom Jesus himself called to share his life. Judas betrayed him. Peter denied knowing him. And the rest fled at his moment of need and stayed hidden out of fear. They had forgotten his firm assertion that he was to be put to death, and even when presented with the word of eyewitnesses, they would not accept his Resurrection, which he had also said would come about. So are not we, who never heard his voice or looked into his eyes, just as capable of turning our back on Jesus?

When someone begins to be very acutely aware of the goodness of God, the desire to do his will becomes of utmost importance. For some, unfortunately, the fear of sin becomes an obsession. We do not refer to the calculating Catholic asking: "Father, would it be a mortal sin if I...?" A saint, however, truly wants to please God and is not motivated by the "fear" of punishment. The "fear" of the saint is to be a disappointment to the one who died on the cross for love.

Holiness is, after all, an intimate bond of love with the Creator, which sin contradicts. To think of holiness only in terms of doing good leaves it on the level of intelligence and not of the will. To determine never to do what is wrong may constitute a moral life, but it does not make one holy. A person who practices no religion, or does not even believe in God, can live by a moral code. But never to insult, lie to or steal from a friend does not in any shape or form prove that we are filled with love. Our affection demands positive acts of goodness from us, without looking for recompense. Love is a free gift of "time, talent or treasure," maybe all three. The good we do is called virtue and goes beyond morality. Virtue leads us to holiness, since it is the pathway to justice on behalf of our neighbors and our society. More importantly, that is what Jesus expects of us.

More than a voice in the ear

The first steps that we took on our spiritual journey, many years ago, might have been made with the effort to tread carefully through the minefield of sin. Our concern was how to avoid the punishment of hell. We were determined to follow our conscience, to do what was right, not to offend God. Our wish to avoid the punishments of hell may have even caused us a period of anxiety, plagued with the scourge of scruples. But somewhere along the line, we must put aside the fear of committing sin and be more determined to love God and neighbor, namely to do good. By this time our conscience has moved, let us hope, from the concern of punishment to the desire to please the beloved, our Lord Jesus.

Let us take time to review the differences between spiritual growth and the simple fulfillment of moral principles. Physical realities determine our decisions concerning material things. They are relatively easy to come by, since they are based on common sense or scientific evidence. If we ignore the laws of nature, which have been determined by God, we will eventually learn that to do so has dire consequences. Some are immediate. Others are more long-range.

Moral judgments, on the other hand, flow from our spiritual nature, which we have as creatures made in the image of God with consequent responsibilities for each other. An intrinsic part of the spirit is our intellect. Application of our intelligence to a moral choice is called *conscience*. To base a moral judgment on what feels better and not on what is right betrays our rational nature. Its effects may not be immediate, but eventually it will affect our relationship to others and often impair our health. Guilt will eventually win out.

This built-in mechanism by which we determine whether our actions are good or bad, virtuous or evil, is a response to a standard that our reason recognizes. Our conscience cannot be ignored, for it is the function of our reasoning powers. Hence, if we do not wish to feel guilty about our selfish choices, it is necessary to deny the existence of an absolute standard. This, of course, is the ultimate form of relativism and demands that our conscience be silenced.

Society needs laws (termed *civil*) to keep order and provide for the common good. Since there are evil people abroad, government enacts *criminal* laws to protect its citizens. Yet with more laws than ever and more lawyers per capita than anywhere in the world to interpret and enforce the laws, the United States should be the most moral nation in the world. It is probably more true that an abundance of laws is more an indication that immorality is king. Unfortunately, the time comes in an immoral society when laws will be enacted to protect from civil consequences those who have chosen evil. The United States has arrived at the place where civil laws are in place that are contrary to the right order to which nature's God has called us.

We have come to accept the sad fact that our national conscience has been silenced by society's call for tolerance, by the standard of expediency that prevails today. Guilt is a bad word. Christians beware! We must be alert to this sophistry of our age. Reason still rules, and, where faith enters in, our choices must be based on gospel values. We are often called upon to choose, not between good and evil, but between something that is good and something that is better.

Where doubt is present when we are faced with a moral decision, the question that will cut through the confusion raised up by our social environment remains: "What does Jesus expect of me?" In this way we let the love of God drive us.

Sin is just under the surface.

Saints eventually learn a healthy respect for their own weakness and their propensity toward prideful motivations. They soon overcome any self-serving confidence that they are beyond ever seriously betraying Jesus. This is accomplished only by maintaining a healthy consciousness that the fundamental relationship we all have to Jesus is one of Redeemer and redeemed, joined to a respect for and frequent use of the sacrament of reconciliation. Past sins, present confusion and future temptations are never far from consciousness. In fact, many who are given great responsibilities for the glory of God and the salvation of souls approach this tribunal of forgiveness often, even weekly.

To strengthen oneself against temptation may be considered a negative motive for "going to confession." Our weakness does require, however, the steady influence of the grace of confession. Indeed, we know that sanctity is not a matter of simply avoiding sin, but rather of pursuing a life of virtue. Hence, we confess frequently lest the very good we do is minimized because our motivation is less than perfect. It is possible to do good deeds for the wrong reason, or to deny God the credit for the good we do. Saints constantly remind themselves that God is the source of all that is good.

Confession is not an easy exercise for human beings. We are inclined to go only when we sense that "it has been too long." Also, its frequent use might suffer from a casual routine and therefore become almost useless for spiritual progress. To advance in holiness demands the good use of this sacrament. So we begin by declaring that the act of confessing is not something that we should ever enjoy, or find easy. Do you remember your youthful experience with "going to confession"?

This story told of Al Smith might remind you. In 1928 he was the first Catholic to be nominated by a major party for president of the United States. One Saturday evening, while he was governor of New York, he was standing in line for confession at a church in Albany near the state capitol. The man next to the confessional noticed that the governor was standing right behind him. He made a noble gesture. "Governor Smith," he said, "you are a busy man. I would like you to take my place. I have time to wait." The governor demurred. "Thank you very much," he said. "But I am no more anxious to go in there than you are."

My memory of waiting on a confessional line as a young man is still with me. My trepidation mounted as I got nearer to the curtain. "Would the priest be *easy*?" I always wondered if I would say too much or not enough. Looking back from the advantage of age and years of hearing confessions myself, I realize it was fear of the unknown (the priest) or normal self-consciousness that complicated a basically simple procedure.

For some, confession is still like a visit to the dentist, necessary but not relished. Only the knowledge that it will produce a great feeling of relief and peace afterward gives them the fortitude to go forward. What one does in receiving this sacrament is essentially "to make an apology to God for disappointing him and to ask his forgiveness" through his representative, the priest. This simple understanding can be lost sight of when we struggle with an exaggerated sense of guilt that focuses our attention on the "pains of hell."

Confession is no laughing matter.

A penitent would find little or no humor in his confession of sins, although a confessor might try it as a last resort to dispel the anxieties of a person obsessed with scrupulosity. For the penitent, the acknowledgment of one's sinfulness is a very serious matter. The same holds for the priest who often finds himself humbled as the divine instrument in the return of a sinner to God's love. But even in the "devotional" confession, so called because it does not involve mortal sins, a priest will sometimes sense that he is confessing a saint, given the intensity of the sorrow and purpose of amendment not to offend God and to imitate Jesus more faithfully in love of neighbor. On occasion, however, he also finds something to smile about in the confessional.

I recall an incident that concerned a young girl who was very nervous because it was her first confession. She was able to remember everything that she had been taught. She confessed her sins, and after a few words of encouragement the priest said softly: "For your penance you will say three Hail Marys." Silence. Then she burst into tears. "What's the trouble, little one?" he asked sympathetically. "Father," she sobbed, "I know only *one* Hail Mary."

For the penitent (and for the priest most of the time) confession is a very serious business. To admit wrongdoing to another human being (even though unknown and bound by the strictest of all confidences) is no easy thing. A sincere intention to amend one's life is a necessity, and the word of the penitent would be very rarely questioned. It is in one's best spiritual interest to be honest with the confessor, and the priest will not presume otherwise. But the preparation for every confession must sincerely address the angle of future intent in order to advance in virtue toward the goal of holiness. Confession is not the place for routine spirituality. Every person's relationship to God is unique, and a confessor considers each person special. In our own reception of the sacrament, none of us should think otherwise.

Confession will never be "fun." But it should not be difficult. The best way to make it "easy" is to do it often, at least, if possible, every two months. Then we will only need to acknowledge those venial sins that we want to focus on. When the sacrament of reconciliation is seen not just as the way to have one's sins forgiven, but also as an "encounter with Christ," it becomes very strengthening and will spur us on to a more personal response to his love.

No ground between sin and virtue

From the garden of Eden, sin has been part of our human condition. Pride was possible even to Adam and Eve, those first perfect beings who were endowed with intelligence and free will and were free of carnal passion. They were expelled from paradise because they wanted to do their own will. For their sin of pride human beings lost the state of innocence. Thus we are all born in sin. At the present time we are capable of being restored to grace and the love of God, because Jesus our Savior redeemed us by his death on the cross. As our Savior, he satisfied the justice of his Father, but we still remain subject to all the temptations of our fallen nature.

With all the weaknesses of the flesh that we are heir to, we must not forget, as we pursue a life of holiness, that the fundamental cause of sin and the obstacle to sanctity is our own pride, the refusal to do what God expects of us. Our will, not the divine will, seeks to guide our actions. This, of course, is the antithesis of love. Everyone knows the broad parameters of what God wants from us through the Ten Commandments given to Moses. Christians certainly know more because of the truth brought to us by Jesus as revealed in the Gospels and throughout the New Testament.

So the path to holiness is outlined in the Word of God, and every plan toward that end must begin there. Let us not imitate the man who becomes frustrated with his attempts to assemble the tricycle that he has bought for his son and can get nothing to work. He is best advised to read the instructions. How applicable to us human beings when we find ourselves upset with our life's circumstances, and our efforts to be holy fall short of expectations. Too often we do not realize that we are ignoring the owner's manual, until our lives get unhinged. For us, the Holy Scriptures are our books of instructions. Yet, even when we turn to

God our Creator for answers, our attitude often goes awry. We demand that God straighten everything out by direct intervention, instead of turning to the directions he has already laid out for us in the Bible.

In the Book of Exodus we have a summary of his "directions for assembly," namely, the Ten Commandments. We have guidance throughout the Hebrew Scriptures, especially in the Wisdom books, such as Sirach. More particularly as Christians, the New Testament, especially in the Gospels, has very pointed warnings and counsels for us. The directions that Jesus offers for long-lasting happiness and peace are often ignored. They frequently revolve around the difficult virtues of justice and mercy, which separate anyone who sincerely desires holiness from those who simply want to "feel holy."

The virtue of justice can refer directly to God as an expression of faith, such as reverence and adoration, the opposing vices being blasphemy and superstition. In daily life, however, justice concerns our responsibilities to fellow human beings. Each of us has rights given by the Creator that call for recognition by all others. The right to life is owed to every child of God. These encompass many areas, including the right to be treated with courtesy and the chance for work, housing, education and health care. We directly violate justice when we deny people opportunities to live in dignity, but also when we just do not care enough to lend a necessary hand where we can. Saints strive to love God and also to love their neighbor without considering each act of love as a distinct effort.

Jesus' death on the cross has repaired the damage that was done to divine justice through sin. Thus we are in a position to receive the mercy of God, to try again. His justice demands that we respect each other and ourselves, since everyone has been created by him and belongs to him. For those who stubbornly ignore God's "instruction manual" and obstinately hang on to their own selfishness, only "time in purgatory" (or the fires of hell) will satisfy the divine justice. But saints recognize that there is an alternative—to accept the Father's offer of a "share in the cross of Jesus" by daily suffering of body or spirit. They do not waste any opportunity to accept these chances to advance on the journey toward union with the Blessed Trinity through union with the cross of Jesus. With each confession, having received the mercy of a loving Father by an admission of guilt within the sacrament of reconciliation and an expression of sorrow with the intention of accepting the reparations offered, saints continue to proceed steadily and joyfully on their challenging journey.

Being sorry is not enough.

Progress in virtue is not made simply by acknowledging that I have sinned. The cause of the sin must be rooted out. Those who would be holy may wonder why they still commit sin. They ask: "Can I perhaps confess more sincerely?" They are never satisfied that they are being totally faithful. Are we perhaps still in the first stages of conversion and more focused on avoiding sin than in practicing virtue?

"But I already said that I was sorry." Remember that plaintive plea when your mother grounded you for the mistreatment of a younger sibling or other misdeed? You figured that an apology would get you off the hook, with no punishment. Those in the public domain who are trying to please others seem never to get beyond juvenile thinking. "I am sorry," has become a familiar response from certain celebrities, notably those of the sports world and some politicians. It often begins: "If I have offended anyone..." This latter phrase does not even indicate guilt, but is more an acknowledgment of thoughtlessness at best and stupidity at worst. To admit guilt means that I fully intended to do something that I knew was wrong.

The expression "I am sorry" is especially suspect if one was brought to contrition only after being caught and is afraid of losing something that is held dear, namely, a position, money, freedom or a person whom one has loved. That is not sorrow so much as remorse.

But we Catholics, as would-be saints, know about true sorrow (*contrition*) much better than most. We say to God "I am sorry" as part of the sacrament of reconciliation when we admit that we have sinned, and these words are implied when we say at the beginning of Mass: "Lord, have mercy." We believe that sorrow for sin is an essential ingredient in our relationship to God as his redeemed people.

Yet, we may wonder why we do not improve even after sincere confession of sins with the intent to sin no more. The problem may be that we forget there is more to true sorrow than simply the admission that "I have sinned," even if that includes a purpose of amendment. I must be a *repentant* sinner, one who is willing to undo the damage my sin has caused another (restitution) and to accept the consequences inherent to my sin. But it goes beyond that if we wish to become holy. We must look to initiate our own

BETRAYAL

penalties when none flow directly from the sin (*repa-ration*). An awareness rooted in our belief that we have been redeemed by the death of the Son of God will prompt us to strengthen the bonds of love that exist between ourselves and those whom we have offended.

"Then he began to reproach the cities in which most of his deeds of power had been done, because they did not repent. 'Woe to you, Chorazin! Woe to you, Bethsaida! For if the deeds of power done in you had been done in Tyre and Sidon, they would have repented long ago in sackcloth and ashes...'" (Matthew 11:20–21).

Hence, after confession we need to cover ourselves in the *sackcloth of restitution* and the *ashes of reparation* if the angels of heaven are to rejoice over this repentant sinner.

The many faces of sin

Not one of us is free from the effects of original sin, although we have been restored to grace by baptism. There continues to exist within us an attraction toward sin because of our fallen nature. These tendencies have been labeled the *capital sins,* because every type of sin can be traced to them. They pull against the spirit of God.

These sources of sin are generally classified into two groups. First are those obsessions that are more easily recognized as the source of temptation, since they find a basis in our *physical* nature. They are stimulated from the outside. The temptations in the second group are subtle, since they come from within us, that is, from our *spiritual* nature. The danger comes from the ability of our intelligence and will to justify their fulfillment with some ease.

The legitimate requirements of our corporal being are readily seen to be prone to excess. We have a need for clothing, housing, transportation, tools for work, and so forth. If the desire to possess is allowed free rein, we will become entrapped by *covetousness*, which begets sins of simple thievery or the more subtle forms of stealing such as insurance fraud or cheating in the workplace. By the practice of generosity, ready to help those in need, we can prevent an absorption by materialism and the greed it engenders.

We also have a healthy physical attraction for sexual bonding and commitment that reflects every normal and healthy aspect of being men or women. By the nature we have from God, our human destiny is marriage, and so we recognize the dignity and power that abides in the union of body and spirit that makes up the human person. In our disordered nature, however, *lust* begets fornication, adultery, homosexuality or sexual abuse of oneself or others. Only by chastity in thought and modesty in dress and behavior are we able to discipline the attraction for people and places that promote unruly sensuality.

Both covetousness and lust are the most powerful deviations that flow from our corporal needs. Combined with the need to control others, they may go beyond the expression of the physical to become an intellectual *lust for power*.

Our physical nature also requires food and drink to maintain life with the strength to work. Such appetites provide legitimate pleasure as a gift of God. But no one doubts that we easily eat more of what we enjoy to the detriment of our health and use to excess alcohol or other drugs in order to ease life's pressures. Such tendency is termed *gluttony,* and we must practice temperance in the enjoyment of the sensual appetite as well as the mortification of these physical desires. Fasting and abstinence have the additional benefit of sharpening the mind, and they support the spirit of prayer.

In addition to this need of providing sustenance for the health of our bodies, we must also sleep and take time to relax so as to refresh our spirit. Also beneficial will be an occasional extended period of rest or simple diversion. At times the last thing we want to think about is work. To maintain a balance between responsibility and recreation, we must remain attentive to the people for whom we are most responsible and always consider first what is best for them.

Sloth (laziness) affects our spiritual health also, since our attention is put on the here and now, away from our relationship to God.

Because sin flows from our animal nature, we are readily aware when our temptation is to carnal excess. We are easily on the alert. We are, however, prone to excess even in those areas which flow from our dignity as creatures of intellect and will, made to the image of God. Thus we have an innate sense of justice and human rights and for the proper order required between individuals, families, communities and nations. But in selfish focus upon *our* personal interests, or those of *our* family, *our* community or *our* country, we easily succumb to the defensive excesses of pride, anger and envy.

Pride in one's own dignity and accomplishments fuels a sense of competition always to be the best. When contested, this may generate into lies, unreasonable demands, violent speech or actions, etc., which are fueled by *anger* and often prolonged by *envy*. The latter flows from an exaggerated feeling that another person has what should rightfully be mine. Conversely, when I sense that something I already possess (things, position, dignity, respect) is in danger of being co-opted by another, the ugly specter of *jealousy* complicates the equation. If we exercise courtesy in our dealings with each individual whom we encounter, which is basic charity, we will banish any sense of superiority, the enemy of all virtue.

Begone, Satan!

In the garden of Gethsemane, when Jesus returned to the Apostles who were asleep, he said: "Stay awake and pray that you may not come into the time of trial; the spirit indeed is willing, but the flesh is weak" (Matthew 26:41). We see that Jesus is totally aware that, when personal danger of any kind lurks, we will be open to the cowardly act.

Jesus has also shown us the way to handle our temptations. Before he began his public life of preaching, he "was led up by the Spirit into the wilderness to be tempted by the devil" (Matthew 4:1). There he was subjected to three distinct temptations: one to sensuality (v. 3), one to presumption (v. 6) and one to power (v. 9). These comprise the three areas in which we, too, are tempted.

When Jesus was hungry, he was tempted to sensuality, "If you are the Son of God, command these stones to become loaves of bread" (Matthew 4:3). He replied: "One does not live by bread alone, but by every word that comes from the mouth of God" (Matthew 4:4).

After Satan took him to the parapet of the temple, he was tempted to sin by presumption: "If you are the Son of God, throw yourself down; for it is written, 'He will command his angels concerning you,' and 'on their hands they will bear you up, so that you will not dash your foot against a stone'" (Matthew 4:6). Jesus answered: "Again it is written, 'Do not put the Lord your God to the test'" (Matthew 4:7).

Finally, from the top of a mountain, he faces the subtle temptation to power when the devil showed him all the kingdoms of the world and suggested, with shameless arrogance: "All these things I will give you, if you will fall down and worship me" (Matthew 4:9). Jesus responded: "Away with you Satan! For it is written, 'Worship the Lord your God, and serve only him'" (Matthew 4:10).

In these three areas of temptation, we will recognize our own attractions to sin. Lust and gluttony make us susceptible to sensuality (self-indulgence). Pride, envy and sloth lead to presumption (of God's grace). Anger and covetousness feed our desire for power (even to accomplish good). All of us can readily see that we are not tempted with the same degree of intensity in each area. Some we control easily. Others we keep at bay only by a strong regimen of prayer and fasting.

Jesus shows us the way to handle them all. The devil does not fool him. He knows the origin of the temptations, even though they are clothed with "goodness." About sensuality: everything you desire is a gift from God; all your natural appetites and impulses are good. About presumption: God is good; trust him to protect you and he is always ready to forgive you. About power: your talents are from God; he wants you to be the first to enjoy the fruit of your work.

So the first need is to learn to recognize temptation for what it is at the very moment it surfaces. We must never forget that the basic weakness of human nature is to rationalize any action for our own advantage. (Remember Adam in the garden of Eden.) A fight with temptation is a no-winner. The devil wants us to fight him, because he always comes out on top. He wins whether we succumb or whether we are just wounded. Jesus showed us that the only defense was to flee from the temptation, to reject the tempter. In practice this means that we immediately run away from the person, place or circumstance that is attracting us, with the speed we would withdraw our hand from a flame the moment we are aware of its closeness.

God is not finished with you yet!

The Apostles asked Jesus why he spoke in parables. His answer was: "To you has been given the secret of the kingdom of God, but for those outside, everything comes in parables; in order that 'they may indeed look, but not perceive and may indeed listen, but not understand; so that they may not turn again and be forgiven'" (Mark 4:11–12).

We know that God always answers prayers and that sometimes his answer is "no," because our request will not be spiritually beneficial to us or perhaps not helpful to someone else. However, when we ask for a totally unselfish good, we expect that the answer should be positive and immediate. One example would be the prayers we send heavenward for the conversion of a good friend, that he should return to the practice of his faith. We find it incomprehensible that a God who is omnipotent and loves us does not respond immediately to our very reasonable request.

But experience soon teaches us that besides deep faith and trust in God, we also need a lot of patience. We are sure that he has his own good reasons for delay. But what possible purpose could that be?

Let us think about that. Would we ask a favor of someone who has refused us in the past? Then why should God? God knows beforehand whether a person will say yes or no. Hence we might say that he will not *waste* grace with a direct assault on people who are not yet ready to respond with a generous "yes." Be assured, however, that he will be coaxing them along. How many years did he make Saint Monica wait until he showered grace on her son, Saint Augustine?

In the past when we learned that someone was praying for us (maybe to overcome a bad habit or do better in school) did we improve on the spot? Yet prayer is never wasted energy. The grace "reserved" for us will come into play when we are ready to respond to God's call to deeper holiness, perhaps to a life of heroic virtue.

Let us remember that Jesus did not press his teaching on others. Because the people were not yet disposed to accept the Good News of salvation, he taught in parables. Some, like the Pharisees, were hostile; others were more interested in what he could do for them, perhaps cure a sickness. We are not unlike them in many ways.

With the wisdom of those who are already "of the kingdom," we should understand. God waits until he has someone ready to respond to the grace that has been won by another's prayer. He will act in his own good time and not be rushed by the likes of us.

To focus on avoiding sin is always a mistake. To put it rather plainly, no one becomes holy because he does not sin. Virtue is the expression of charity, and charity is love in action. Since God has loved us first, we are returning his love by our charity toward others, since we cannot do anything directly for God. To live for oneself is self-love, which is sinfulness.

CHAPTER SIX

the game plan of virtues

This is my commandment, that you love one
another as I have loved you.
—John 15:12

Before we set out on a journey, we want to be
clear about our destination and exactly how we are
going to arrive there. Any goal we set for our life also
must have a plan of action toward the attainment of
our purpose. Equally important is our journey to sainthood and the goal of holiness. A blueprint is needed to
show the relationship of the parts to the whole, what is
required for sanctity. These parts are called virtues;
that is, the various actions that reflect the love we
have for God and neighbor. Obviously, holiness is more
than doing penance and staying away from sin.
Indeed, sin is a negative to be avoided and penance is
a necessary cleaning up process. On the other hand,
mortification is a bulwark against sin and a preparation for the practice of virtues, which are positive acts
of goodness. They are love in the concrete.

Traditionally, virtues have been classified into *the-*
ological, those that pertain to our relationship with

God; and *moral* or *cardinal*, those that refer to our relationship with our neighbor. But you cannot practice what you do not understand. Hence, I present this review as a plan of action.

Can the blind have a favorite color?

The road toward sainthood is indeed a way that can be viewed only for a very short distance and cannot be seen with the eyes of the body, that is, be understood from experience or by reason. The journey is spiritual, whose hills and valleys, turns and forks, are seen only through the eyes of faith. The way becomes clearer as the power of faith strengthens. To live by faith is to know something through the gift of spiritual insight, which is beyond our human capabilities, physical or intellectual. Let us be sure that we understand this.

Little children sometimes feel that a thing exists only if it can be seen. Remember when in our very young days we closed our eyes with the expectation that the ugly thing that we were looking at would disappear? As a youngster, did you ever say to someone: "I'm not looking at you, so you might as well go away?" Yet we know that something does not exist because we can see it, but we see it because it exists. God exists, and he loves us. But we can know this love only if he gives us the power to believe in him (faith), later to trust in his promises (hope) and then to be able to experience his love and to love him in return (charity).

In the Gospels we read of the many times Jesus cured people who were blind. They had never known the beauty of colors or responded to the smile of a loved one. He seems to have performed such miracles to demonstrate the need of spiritual sight. By our natural condition we cannot know, trust or love God. For we, too, were born blind, that is, unable to "see" because we are born without the power of faith.

To accept on the Word of God what the human senses cannot discern or what human reason cannot understand is the gift of "sight" received through the sacrament of baptism. Through the sacrament of maturity, which is confirmation, we learn not only to *see* but also to *understand* what we see. We are given the strength to fulfill what that faith demands of us. Thus we do not fear to act on what we believe, even when God's goodness is very difficult to comprehend from a human perspective. Thus we discover the fruit of faith that is the sign of holiness, namely, the spirit of peace. Our trust in God increases and love intensifies. We grow in love because we refuse to close the eyes of faith. We do not want his will to disappear.

Although faith is a virtue that is theological, that is, is directed toward God himself, it does not separate us from our relationship to people. In fact, most of its practical application will involve people. The world is full of individuals with whom we are not comfortable, because of their personalities, their attitudes or even their sinfulness. Yet our belief in the goodness of God our Creator demands that we do not look away, but look upon them with eyes of faith. Meanwhile, we will see in them what God sees in them, and we will not fear to make them part of our lives. Only rarely will we encounter those who make the devil rejoice. In such a case they are best left to God.

By faith we "see" with the eyes of God, and a saint strives to see only with divine eyes. Jesus demands that we not be selective about whom we will love, since he died for all. Yet, our sinfulness will prompt us to look only at the nice people whom we meet and close our eyes to the rest, hoping that they will not be there when we open them again. Saints know that this is not childlike, but childish.

Living on promises

On any trip we may find it helpful to stop for a breather, or at least for a chance to evaluate our progress toward our destination. Time has come for a few reflections lest we begin to wonder whether our holiness journey is worth the effort. This can happen when the trials that will inevitably come are sapping our energies and making us discouraged. We might even be feeling sympathetic to Job who lamented: "Let the day perish in which I was born, and the night that said, 'A man-child is conceived'" (Job 3:3).

Let's ask ourselves a few questions. Why were we born in this place at this time and not in another country or in another century? Only God knows why, and he is not saying. Also, what if the world had come to an end in the last century? If that had been God's plan, the fact is plain that we would never, not ever, have existed. Nor would we have known the difference.

Now that we are experiencing the reality of being alive, two notions are disturbing to our rational nature; namely, never to have existed, and to revert to nothingness when we die. But the fact remains that we have received the gift of life and, indeed, the gift of life into eternity as well. Death is really the passageway from one life to another. If that life would be in hell for eternity, then annihilation would be a reasonable wish. The thought that in place of eternal joy we have chosen such never-ending horror would be totally unbearable. Then Job's lament would be appropriate. That is the awfulness of freedom. Called to love and to be loved (which is the essence of a spiritual life), it is possible to live selfishly, to reject love. But just as we did not choose life, neither can we choose annihilation at our death.

But the hope of an eternal life in heaven is ours because we have been reborn through the sacrament of baptism. Thus beyond our natural life we share the life of God himself, Father, Son and Holy Spirit, and as adopted children the promise to inherit eternal joy with God. Yet our supernatural life (beyond the order of our nature) is also a gift from God and, difficult to realize, *might not have been,* except for the death and Resurrection of Jesus.

Our consciousness makes us aware that we are indeed alive, here and now, and are someone who had never lived before. Through baptism we have also received the gift of God's own life and its promises. This divine life in us has matured (confirmation), been nourished regularly (Holy Eucharist) and our strength has been renewed by rest and an occasional cure (reconciliation). Our faithfulness to God as his adopted children will bring us to eternal joy.

That is why it's a wonderful life! So, unlike Job, we bless the day we were born and the day of our rebirth. We praise the good God, author of life, as we wait for the day that we pass to an everlasting life, one of perfect love. Fear of future difficulty confounds only those who have no hope. Saints trust that the goodness of their heavenly Father will never fail.

Don't look down!

The standard advice given to a patient the day after an uncomplicated operation usually runs along this vein: "The worst is over. Each day you will be feeling better." I suppose that for the most part this is true, and we are buoyed up by a good prognosis. Yet there are other occasions when we hear the old saw of discouragement: "Things get worse before they get better." Saints know that there are better days ahead, perhaps far ahead, but also are aware, from the promises of Jesus, that the immediate future may very well be tough indeed.

Despair is the condition of a soul that feels no hope whatsoever over a present difficulty. In human situations, which mostly depend on the good will of others as well as our own sincere best efforts, which are often found lacking, loss of hope can be understandable. It is even possible to comprehend why those who have been cut off from the awareness of God's love would choose the alternative of suicide.

Perhaps we are most crushed when we have been longing for something wonderful that is within our reach, and expected success turns into profound disappointment. Some examples would be the anticipation of a monetary windfall to bring us out of debt, freedom after a period of confinement or the finding of a true love. Unfortunately, most of these are based on a wish, rather than on the hope of something promised us. Contentment before the fact depends on the strength of our trust in someone whom we know has the power to deliver on a promise.

From all accounts in the Gospels, Mary of Magdalene, the Apostles and all the other disciples were devastated when Jesus was put to death. Yet Jesus had strongly indicated several times that he would undergo punishment and death at the hands of the scribes and elders and given assurance to his followers that he would rise to life again on the third day. Why did they not remember?

Even when we know that the sun will rise in the morning, a sleepless night filled with pain can make it very difficult to remain joyful. True, but it need never destroy our expectation of a good day ahead. That is why a Christian seeking holiness, no matter how much the passion of Jesus is part of life, does not despair like those who have no hope. We believe in the Resurrection of Jesus, that in conquering death he assured us of a share with him in eternal life. We truly expect that there are better days ahead.

The anticipation of again being with those whom we loved on earth should give us strength to bear the disappointments, pains and other trials of this life, patiently carrying the cross of Christ so as not to be left out in the Resurrection on the last day. I often think of the gentleman whom I had just informed that the doctor was certain he had but two or three days to live. He smiled, and with a twinkle in his eye asked me, "Is anyone up there that you want me to give your regards to?" It was the only time I met him, but I knew from only fifteen minutes that I was watching a saint die.

There are no lazy saints.

God's promise of love is for all eternity. Here in our earthly sojourn, we must prove ourselves worthy of it. Although nothing we do can add to God's glory, we ourselves can grow closer to him each time we give thanks for his goodness and accept his will without complaining, and each time we do good for the others whom he also loves. "Those who say, 'I love God,' and hate their brothers or sisters, are liars; for those who do not love a brother or sister whom they have seen, can not love God whom they have not seen" (1 John 4:20).

As preschool children we were expected to spend a lot of time at play. As we grew older, there came responsibilities with each passing year (especially school work), and our times for play had to be limited. It is called *the maturing process*. As fully grown people we have had to concern ourselves with the welfare of others. This necessitated that we put most of our time into work. Indeed, Scripture says: "...anyone unwilling to work should not eat" (2 Thessalonians 3:10).

Even where physical, emotional and intellectual growth develops in an orderly manner, spiritual maturity often lags behind because of our sinfulness. Just as there are adults with well-developed bodies and minds who avoid work like a plague, so in the spiritual order there are Christians who will use every excuse not to act spiritually mature, even after they have received confirmation, the sacrament of maturity. Allow me to illustrate with an incident I once read about.

One Sunday morning a couple was hurrying to church for Mass. While still several blocks away they saw an elderly gentleman slip on the ice and fall. He seemed hurt and was having a very difficult time getting to his feet. "Stop the car, George," the wife insisted. "We must help that man!" Her husband kept driving. "If we do that," he said, "we will be late for Mass."

That story easily makes us think of the question that Jesus asked of the scheming Pharisees: "Is it lawful to cure on the sabbath?" And then he would do just that. His explanation was simple: "The sabbath was made for humankind, and not humankind for the sabbath" (Mark 2:27). Charity is the first law of the Christian life. We cannot use a positive command ("Keep holy the Sabbath day") to excuse ourselves from assisting a neighbor in need. In the situation described above, the couple's first duty was charity. The husband used the responsibility for attending Mass on Sunday as an excuse to avoid getting involved.

On the other hand, charity can never be an excuse for doing something forbidden by God ("Thou shalt not..."). Immature Christians sometimes ignore such negative commands in order to do a perceived good. They have the misconception that the end does justify the means. (Abortion is the easiest example to cite.) There can be no excuse for doing what contradicts God's plan for his creation. We term such actions *evil*.

No one would want to be known as a lazy person. Yet, notwithstanding the grace of confirmation, we often overlook our spiritual childishness. Even a saint may be tempted to juggle priorities, either to work so hard that prayer is put in second place or to neglect responsibilities of charity in order to spend "more time with God." Each is a different form of laziness.

Staying connected

"I feel your pain" has become a trite phrase to express one's compassion, a word that indeed does mean "suffering with." Like so many other bits of conventional wisdom, this one is also not exactly true. No one can really feel another's pain unless he or she has suffered in the exact same way, such as the death of a child, the loss of one's eyesight, the agony of arthritis and so on. The converse, however, is true. Unlike pain, we can "feel the joy" of another if the cause affects us the same way. We can *share* joy; pain is our own.

But we can suffer with another in the sense of being there when someone needs us. That is really what we all desire when we are in pain of heart or body, since to suffer totally alone can be the greatest misery. To stand by a sick bed, to go to a wake or funeral, to stand near a friend who is afraid is what "suffering with" is all about. But in reality, we must do our own suffering. No one else can really understand, or feel, what we are going through. In that same sense we all die alone.

Jesus understands all this. On the night before he died, following the Last Supper, he left for the garden of Gethsemane to join in prayerful union with the Father as his soul anticipated the coming hours of humiliation and beatings. He also knew the dread of the agonizing death on the cross that he would suffer the following day. But he did not want to be alone. "I am deeply grieved, even to death; remain here, and stay awake with me" (Matthew 26:38). Because the Apostles fell asleep, he expressed his disappointment: "So, could you not stay awake with me one hour?" (Matthew 26:40).

For all of us, anticipation enhances the pain or the joy. Looking forward to a vacation trip spreads the joy to the weeks that precede it, and awaiting an operation becomes more agonizing as the date for entering the hospital draws near. We want to have others "feel our joy." But pain we are reluctant to talk about, because it cannot really be shared. We are pleased, however, when a friend or family member stands by. We do not want to be alone when we suffer.

Whatever its value, human comfort goes only so far. We may not be alone, but we suffer alone. Jesus knew the agony of physical pain and even the spiritual pain of betrayal by a friend. He experienced the loneliness of suffering and sought the comforting presence of his Apostles in the garden of Gethsemane. We can expect that he will comfort us when we come to him, because he truly understands "what we are going through."

In the reality of our lives, holiness calls us to be for others as Jesus is for each of us. We seek to share with Jesus his sufferings on Calvary or to appreciate the joys of his home life in Nazareth by being present to our brothers and sisters in their joys and sorrows. A life of charity, as the essence of holiness, very often comes down to a matter of being present, supportive and nonjudgmental.

Foolishness comes in two sizes.

The insult that curdles the psyche of any rational person is the insinuation that one is a fool, which can translate into being downright stupid. A person who is ignorant is only dumb, and we are all ignorant about a lot of things. To make decisions concerning something that one has only limited knowledge about, however, is to act stupidly. To be informed about the important things of life and to make intelligent judgments is demanded by our rational nature. We rise above the vegetable and animal kingdoms, although we share some characteristics of both.

We do not simply grow and develop in one place, as do plants when they have the right combination of soil, water and sunlight, and without which they have no choice but to die where they stand. Animals, on the other hand, move about to seek their food and other needs, and they interact with each other to reproduce, to play or to defend themselves. Their instincts govern them, and they really cannot help themselves to go against the pack. Since their responses are universally predictable, they are not free.

We, however, have intelligence and free will. We are able to take two ideas, compare them, and then come up with a third. We can choose between different possibilities. Animals can fight over food, to maintain their territory, to defend their young. Only human beings can dispute about ideas. But there is a downside. Strictly speaking, only human beings, with their ability to evaluate information and then choose, are able to act stupidly.

We have spoken of the theological virtues that pertain to our relationship with God, which are faith, hope and charity. The virtues that govern our relationship to our neighbors (the *cardinal* virtues) are justice, fortitude and temperance. The fourth is the virtue of prudence, called the "charioteer" virtue because it drives all the others. We are protected from the ultimate stupidity, to trade an eternity of bliss in heaven for earthly fulfillment which is over at death, often much sooner.

On the other hand, even saints can be foolish and in human terms often are. They make their decisions based on spiritual values, which are not accepted by those who consider the values of the present life of greater importance. The worldly wise make their choices in favor of the pragmatic present in a prudent compromise with eternal truth. We only have to think of the circumstances surrounding the death of Saint Thomas More. King Henry VIII and others considered him a fool for maintaining loyalty to his Catholic faith. He accepted the loss of all his earthly goods and power, as well as his life, in a prudent trade for the eternal life of glory in the kingdom of heaven.

With the strength of prudence, we treat our neighbor with dignity as equally called to the happiness of heaven (justice), and we will persevere in doing what is good (fortitude) because of the ultimate goal. The sensuality of our nature will be disciplined (temperance), lest the satisfaction of the moment makes us do stupid things.

A truly prudent person keeps in mind the words said to the rich man who stored up treasure upon treasure: "You fool! This very night your life is being demanded of you. And the things you have prepared, whose will they be?" (Luke 12:20). Saints are prepared to make choices for which they will be called "fool" by friend and foe alike.

I thirst for gratitude.

If one thirsts for water, it means that he lacks water. To thirst for justice is to lack the respect and/or opportunities that are necessary to maintain human dignity. Sanctity is often proved by the efforts made to work for the rights due our neighbor, even when we know that full satisfaction is reached only in eternal life. With divine insight the virtue of prudence recognizes that injustice is more often than not the lot of God's people who live in an environment that is hostile to religion. Jesus himself "thirsted for justice" as he hung on the cross, and those who can identify with Jesus in their own "thirst" will find a powerful impetus toward holiness.

Our relationship to each other as children of God calls for a spirit of gratitude for what we are and have received. Then we can begin to appreciate also the gifts he has bestowed on others and respect them. We begin, of course, with the gift of life itself. This becomes the foundation of the virtue of justice, whereby we respect each person's proper human dignity and rights that have come from God. Among us there ought to be no competition. The first requirement of justice is to be aware that all are dependent on God's goodness and creative power, and we owe it to him to express our thankfulness often. To praise God takes first place in the ranks of justice. A close second is our appreciation for the good we have received from those he sent to help us. Their role as instruments of God should never be taken for granted.

Beginning with our birth itself, we owe everything to God. In addition we have received the promise of eternal joy because the Son of God freely redeemed us from sin by his death on the cross, making us heirs of the kingdom of heaven. So, if we are grateful for that, it carries over into our daily relationship with others who are good to us. Gratitude to God and to those who are our life-support in ways large and small is an integral part of justice and therefore a step toward holiness. We must never take for granted God's goodness to us, often given through those whom he has made part of our lives. When everything is said and done, we can claim only our sins as our own, for which no one deserves thanks.

Gratitude is demanded by the virtue of justice, the extension of a right that is owed. We are obliged to appreciate each other for the favors we receive. It is more than a matter of charity.

Even from a human perspective, gratitude is the oil that makes interpersonal relationships run smoothly. We need other people, in big ways and small, to make life pleasant. Feeling self-sufficient and hence never grateful for what others do for us creates isolation and frustration. Our difficulties cease to be challenges and become obstacles to our peace and insurmountable roadblocks to sanctity.

The saints reached a point where they were even grateful to Jesus for the hard times and pain he allowed them to suffer. They saw such difficulties as a sign of his love, since he trusted them not to complain. By sharing his cross, they were able to draw that much closer to him. This practice of piety (reverence for God and consciousness of his goodness) is the atmosphere in which the flowering of all virtues takes root and which governs our relationship to those who share this world with us.

Courtesy begets goodness.

Persons who are courteous to others are considered nice people. They dare not offend. Rules of etiquette may sometimes be based on culture or local customs, but basically they are simply ways of being respectful of another's sensibilities. Saints are always courteous;

but courtesy alone does not separate saints from sinners. Everything depends on the motivation behind the act of courtesy. To have a reach into eternity, it must be an expression of respect for another, because we accept such a person as having equal dignity before God as we do. Supernatural virtue, simply defined, is the *habit of doing good,* based on the awareness of our common relationship to the God who created us all.

A society of human beings is not just a collection of individuals, but a vibrant organism, whose components are integrally related to many people. There is a web that binds people to each other. Every sin, or evil intention, diminishes our personal worth as intelligent and responsible persons by encouraging our selfishness. Therefore, every bad action, however strictly personal, has an effect on our relationships toward those whom our lives touch. Through them we influence many more. Yet in today's climate there is a readiness to accept the fallacy that private sins ("they don't hurt anyone") have no connection with our public responsibility (morality). To think thus is to misunderstand the cry of justice.

The problem stems from our modern society's failure to place the basis of moral conduct on the acceptance of our nature as coming from God, a reflection of his own image in which we are created. Our first order of business is to give God his due; namely, to believe him when he declares what he expects of us (the Ten Commandments). We are to live by the promise of eternal glory he has made to those who remain faithful and finally to have love for each other as the way we express our love for him.

Although *natural* goodness is possible, that is, virtue based on human instincts of right and wrong, for the most part acquired through the good example of others, we often limit those who benefit from our virtuous acts to *our own kind*. We tend toward personal satisfaction or are inclined to be defensive about what is *ours*. Those who would be holy must remember that virtue can be practiced consistently only when it is based on a belief in God as Father of us all, on trust in his promises to us and on a love that reflects God himself, namely, one which is inclusive, not selective.

Saints, of course, are more interested in the good that they are capable of doing than in the avoidance of harm to others. They may have a concern for "society" at large but their focus is always with each individual that they have contact with even if for only a fleeting moment. They remember that justice forms the foundation of charity and that courtesy to every individual is its cornerstone.

Ever been bored to tears?

Saints are not made in a day, even those who were martyred. They were holy long before their faith was challenged by the threat of death. Sanctity is attained in a long, steady process that calls for the virtue of fortitude, the strength to hang on. Saints are always challenged; they are never bored. Some of us, however, find that on occasion we will surrender to the taunt of the unbeliever that to remain on the cross is a foolish decision. Understanding the evil of sin, the great love of Jesus for us and the wonderful promise of eternal life to those who stay the course is something that the saints accept instinctively.

The adage is so true: "Time flies when you are having fun." When a happy encounter comes to an end, we say: "Where has the time gone?" Or in other words: "I've had a *great* time visiting with you." When celebrating a personal anniversary, we remember the good times and say: "It seems only like yesterday that..." But when we are in the hospital, or in the midst of any painful or distressing situation, like a toothache or an unwelcome guest, we ask: "Will this agony never end?" Of course, we know it will, and so we hang on. We will never do it bravely, however, unless we focus on the agonizing death of Jesus.

Jesus knows our human nature. Look how he prepared Peter, James and John for the horrendous reality of his impending crucifixion by giving them the experience of his Transfiguration, a glimpse of resurrected glory. Yet when the time came for them to face his Passion and death, they, too, forgot their experience and what he had said, that after three days he would arise from the dead.

Our focus on the promise to share eternal glory with him should make suffering with Jesus our pride. In some churches the resurrected Christ has been substituted on the crucifix for the bleeding and agonizing Jesus to encourage us not to forget the connection. However, the saints have all declared that a sharing in Christ's sufferings is the most effective path to holiness. Also the gift of fortitude, based on faith in the Resurrection, will protect against any discouragement.

Saints even find ways to benefit from sermons that propose the means of loving God, but are less than exhilarating. They question themselves on whether they have come to hear what they will like, or if they are prepared for something that may be a harsh directive from God. Most of us, perhaps, can more easily relate to parish Sunday liturgies that fall short of "lifting the spirit." When I hear someone defend why they are avoiding Mass by using these situations as an excuse, I suggest that they go nonetheless, because that is where Jesus wants them to be. They should not forget that at Mass we offer again the sacrifice of Jesus for our sins. Although they might prefer to be elsewhere, the boring experience might help them appreciate more the three interminable painful hours that the Lord was nailed to the cross.

Saints have a way of never losing advantage of any opportunity. They figure that Jesus sometimes allows his disciples to know the true meaning of "bored to death."

The signs of success

Sainthood is a positive condition of the spiritual life, not just a state in which we are no longer bound by sinfulness. Basically holiness demands the doing of good as expressions of our love for God and neighbor. As we have seen, these may come under the categories of specific virtues, which pertain either to God or our neighbor. Toward God we practice faith, hope and charity. Toward neighbor we practice prudence, justice, fortitude and temperance. This latter is best understood under the name of meekness.

Meekness, properly understood, is a fruit of peace. Its practice is not a matter of timidity but of patience. A meek person is one who always has control of his emotional and rational responses and accomplishes good works with a totally spiritual motivation. It proves that one is at least bordering on sainthood.

Perhaps you notice yourself frequently upset and hear yourself praying that most useless of prayers: "O God, please give me patience!" If so, know that you are far from your goal of sainthood. The prayer implies that God could make you "meek and humble of heart" on the spot. That is calling for a complete change in your personality. If your tendency is to be excited about everything, good or bad, you would be asking to be changed into someone new with a more phlegmatic nature, one which has difficulty getting excited about anything.

Patience is not the ability to put up with everything, to be undisturbed by any of life's circumstances. It begins with the awareness that most things are not worth getting upset about, because getting upset does not change anything. Patience is rather the control of one's emotions so as to be clearheaded in order to determine what can be changed, what cannot be changed, and to know the difference. Most often we are responding to other people's disturbing character traits or their thoughtlessness. We are especially affected when their selfishness makes our life more difficult.

So what should we pray for? The simple answer is that we need to ask God for the wisdom to know ourselves, to understand why we expect everything to go our way. We need to realize that many of our own personality traits may be disturbing to others, who may prove to be people exactly like ourselves.

Impatience is actually a form of anger, when we perceive that an injustice is being done to us. When

THE GAME PLAN OF VIRTUES

anger is the response to an injustice being done to another, it is most often justified, and it will be a controlled anger that will accomplish some good. What we seek is the virtue of meekness, to stop becoming annoyed at everything. Serenity is the control of our need to have everything happen now, or even yesterday, in a way that pleases us. To attain this, we must not expect that others will always do what we perceive to be right. The virtue of patience looks beyond the present moment and assures our continued peace. When others do something that pleases us, we will feel happy and not just relieved.

Meekness is a sign of holiness. This is another way of saying that saints are able to take calmly what annoys them, absorb the facts serenely, make proper decisions in charity and then act decisively, all without wanting to be the victor in every battle. This exercise of the Holy Spirit's gift of fortitude reflects courage in the face of adversity, for does not Jesus say: "Blessed are the meek, for they will inherit the earth" (Matthew 5:5)? And this simply means that we will always be in control of our lives in the face of any difficulty or disagreement, and our prayer will not be: "O Lord, give me patience," but will be: "O Lord, deliver me from my foolishness."

CHAPTER SEVEN

dying with Christ

Because he himself was tested by what he suffered, he is able to help those who are being tested.
—Hebrews 2:18

"Ajourney of a thousand miles begins with a single step." This truism holds good also for the spiritual life, which is often described as a journey of faith. This is especially true when one has the intention to become holy. The first step is a change in perspective. Holiness requires more than keeping the commandments and receiving the sacraments on a regular basis. To get as close to God as he will allow requires a definite plan, which will entail at least a change of perspective and for some a complete turnaround. The proper term to express a new sense of values that turns one more directly toward God is *conversion*. We can easily apply this to Augustine of Hippo, who had a steady, albeit dramatic, change in response to grace, or to the sudden jolt of grace in the life of Paul of Tarsus on the road to Damascus. At some point in a

UNTIL THE TRUMPET SOUNDS

saint's life, a conscious decision is made to live only for God, face in a new direction and take a first step in that long journey to holiness.

A new set of values

That first step is a review and possible adjustment of the importance that is attributed to each part of our lives that we have up to the present considered a "value." Distinctions must be made between what may be true values in the area of piety and what may only be our emotional preferences. We must compare each with the basic principles of spiritual development.

A man who enjoys relaxing with a good book considers his quiet time very valuable. For another, nothing is more important after a day's work than sitting down with his family and having supper together. These are all values, but not of equal importance in every circumstance.

We may also speak rightly of religious and moral values, cultural and family values and so forth. We know that varying cultures often perceive family life from differing perspectives, and even persons with no religion can have moral values. It would appear to be futile to speak of "values" and expect common agreement or certitude unless the values are based upon principles. It is a mistake to equate *values* with *principles*, especially when the values are just personal choices. Principles are based on truths, and a value is not a truth. Cultural values are variables, and family values, for example, must go beyond any cultural base and be rooted in firm principle.

Values contradictory to the very principles of human relationships that reside in our nature by the creative will of God are definitely false. The foundation of all Christian life must first acknowledge the relationship to our Creator. Our status as a redeemed people freed from sin by the death of Jesus on the cross calls for us to give high value to a serious life of penance. Without it holiness is impossible.

Thus we can truthfully say that the journey toward holiness is uphill, and the hill is Calvary. Motivated by love to accompany Jesus wherever he goes, we must carry the cross after him without faltering, keep our eyes on the goal and never give any thought to question whether the journey is worth the effort. To do penance for past sins and to practice mortification is fundamental to strengthen us in the face of the subtle and constant attraction to sin. In daily living we each experience different challenges and have different weaknesses. Hence, our sorrow for sin and accompanying penance might call for different practices than the classical *wearing a hair shirt* or *corporal flagellation* practiced by the ancient hermits in the desert. A life of solitude is probably also out of the question.

When our life situation is not already inherently difficult, we should give first preference, when feasible, to the biblical call for fasting, almsgiving and works of charity within modern circumstances. But the basic principle is not concerned with specifics of penance, however valuable, but is the need to live the cross of Jesus intimately. To that cross we touch our values to test their true worth. We must maintain the proper perspective from the hill of Golgotha through the eyes of the suffering Son of God who pleads with us to accept his mercy. This first of spiritual principles, the need of penance and sorrow for sin, gives meaning to all the other aspects of our union with God. Just as a housewife notices the dirty window when the sun shines through it, the awareness that we are truly sinners becomes clearer as we grow closer to the light of God. The brighter the light of God's love penetrates our soul, the more the dark crevices of our spirit are revealed.

Mary carried a cross, too.

Just about all of us, I think, can remember an occasion when we pleaded with a teacher or parish priest or some adult: "Please don't tell my mother." Mothers are special and we want them to think the best of us. There are many things that we might have succeeded in hiding from them, things that we are not proud to look back on. Even if that were the case, we can also remember so many things that we talked over with them, because we knew we could trust them and they would help us with any difficulty when they were able.

As our natural mother was important to our human life in its beginning and its growth, so is Mary, our mother and the mother of Jesus, essential to our growth in holiness. Holiness is being one with Jesus, and that includes Mary. She cannot be separated from Jesus, as the one who was first to share his Passion, since she stood beside the cross and offered him for us. Indeed, no matter how close we might be or have been to our earthly mothers, none of them participates in our adult responsibilities to any extent. We all eventually go on to live our own lives. Not so with the mother of Jesus, who was given to us as the mother of the church. We are her concern always.

Before proceeding we need to contemplate the words about Mary from the Second Vatican Council's *Apostolic Constitution on the Church.*

> The predestination of the Blessed Virgin as Mother of God was associated with the incarnation of the divine word....She conceived, brought forth and nourished Christ; she presented him to the Father in the temple, shared her Son's sufferings as he died on the cross. Thus, in a wholly singular way she cooperated by her obedience, faith, hope and burning charity in the order of grace...which continues uninterruptedly from the consent which she loyally gave at the Annunciation and which she sustained without wavering beneath the cross, until the eternal fulfillment of all the elect. Taken up to heaven she did not lay aside this saving office but by her manifold intercession continues to bring us the gifts of eternal salvation. (Chapter VIII, 61, 62)

Do we need it said any stronger for us to intensify our devotion to Mary and to look to her for our inspiration and strength? The principle is clear. She who offered him from beneath the cross and shared his life intimately from birth to sacrificial death must be part of our life in Jesus. Mary is the mother of the church, his Body, who guided it from the days after his Ascension into heaven, until today as she continues to love us, until we all share her glory in heaven. We must be one with Mary, as Jesus was, for he said to us from the cross through John: "Behold your mother."

As we struggle to walk with Jesus faithfully, we must remember that we are also imitating Mary, who walked with Jesus on the way to Calvary just as she had accompanied him his entire life. She stood beneath the cross and received his lifeless body in her lap. That is our enduring picture of the Sorrowful Mother. We can understand how a human mother suffers when her child suffers and how she is concerned always for her child's welfare, even into adulthood. So we must see Mary as the mother of Jesus suffering with us and caring about us until we are together in heaven with her and with Jesus.

True, we contemplate her glory as Queen of Heaven and praise her beauty and comeliness. But on the journey to holiness, we remember her as the mother of the Redeemer. We need to know her as the mother who willingly shared her son's Passion and death and as the mother who at times weeps over us when we forget. She is the example to us of a mother's love, which keeps focused on the interest of those she loves, renouncing self-interest in all things.

We are always self-centered.

We need all kinds of things to live, things that are helpful only to ourselves. After all, we eat and drink to maintain life; we sleep to renew our strength that we might do our work; we study to prepare ourselves for our life's vocation; we clothe our nakedness and dress warmly in winter so we will not get sick. No one else benefits from these actions, at least directly. Nor do we think of ourselves as selfish for taking care of our health and seeing to our present and future needs. God expects us to do so. And we also cannot survive without people since we are made to love and be loved. Both our physical and spiritual natures are dependent.

The reality is, however, that we often eat and drink too much; we can be lazy and avoid work. Our work can be inspired by ambition for power and possessions. We may dress more elegantly than our state in life demands in order to show up others. We may exploit people for our own interests, rather than love them. Our self-centeredness can be excessive and that, of course, can effectively separate us from any intimacy with Jesus, our Redeemer. We will be content only to avoid sin and get to heaven.

We need to prepare for the journey toward holiness by traveling lightly, by satisfying for sins of the past with penance and by mortifying our sensual and intellectual self-interest. Then we are freed up to receive the grace of the spirit, which is wisdom. Selfishness and love just do not mix. The totally selfish soul is even beyond the love of Jesus, although he will continue to look for some glimpse of goodness.

There must be a balance, of course, because penance and mortification have no value by themselves. They must have a purpose, and the more focused that purpose is, the more will we remove specific obstacles along our path to the perfection of love. And the greater good we sacrifice, the more perfect the love. Perhaps the following story can illustrate how a saint goes about his penitential life. The lesson may be applied broadly.

There was a young priest who enjoyed walking into the school playground after lunch to watch the exuberance of the children and exchange pleasantries with them. There were some who would run over the moment they saw him. One particular second grade girl often led the pack with obvious joy at his attention.

One February day she was not among the adoring crowd. But he noticed her at the other end of the yard. The same thing happened the next day. He was sure that he had unwittingly hurt her feelings and watched for a chance to make up. The opportunity came the following day in the school corridor.

After a greeting, he stated: "I missed you in the yard these last two days. Are you mad at me?" She look flustered and blurted out: "Oh no, Father! Not at all!" Puzzlement made him pause, but he asked: "Then why are you avoiding me?" She hesitated and then said simply: "Because I gave you up for Lent!" "Out of the mouths of babes..." (Psalm 8:2).

You might remember the time when every Catholic gave something up for Lent, especially when unable to fulfill the lenten fast of forty days. This was to ensure detachment from the things that might be hindering our love for God, especially anything that might interfere with our prayer life or distract us from our responsibilities. Maybe, like the girl above, we wanted to show Jesus that we did love him above everything or anyone, beyond the need to do penance for our sins.

Indeed, *fasting* represents the classical form of penance. It can mean giving up food by quantity, but it also includes abstaining from an excess of "good times" however innocent. Of course, nature abhors a vacuum, and so does our super-nature. So any life of penance must include prayer or spiritual reading and, most importantly, working harder to fulfill our responsibilities to family, friends, community and especially where we earn our livelihood. We must try to accept hardships quietly, without complaint, and seek ways to bring some unexpected joy to others, such as answering a long delayed letter.

In Lent, of course, we might wish our penance to express gratitude for the Passion and death of Jesus. We rejoice that we have been freed from our sins and that by reason of his Resurrection we have been promised eternal life. Appreciation for what we have already received is an essential ingredient of love.

But let us finish the story that I began. Upon hearing the answer of the little girl, the priest smiled warmly upon the face of this little Saint Therésè of Lisieux. "But you made me very sad," he said to her. "Why didn't you tell me what you were up to?" The child looked sheepish. "Because," she replied, "Sister said that we should not tell anyone what we give up for Lent. So it was a secret between Jesus and me."

Jesus suffers with us.

The expression "misery loves company" is a way of saying that our human nature finds it difficult to suffer in silence, to be totally isolated in the bad moments of life. A sign of friendship is to share with another his moments of bereavement or disappointment and offer solace by our words or simple presence. That is how love works. We appreciate it and are bolstered by another's concern for us. As we come closer to Jesus on our journey to holiness, we soon learn that we are expected to suffer with him more and more. It becomes our bond. Our strength, however, must come from the realization that Jesus knows what we feel and suffers with us. We need never feel alone in our misery.

An experience that we all have at various times in our lives is the loss of a loved one. For example, many a widow acknowledges, even five or more years after the death of her husband, that she often feels lonely. When the initial pain of separation is relived, the emptiness is felt once again and the eyes fill with tears. Yet, married or not, all of us know the feeling of emptiness at the death of one who has been close to us, whether a parent or a sibling or a good friend. Part of our heart has been ripped away. That is why the Gospel narrative about the raising of the dead Lazarus touches us and is a reminder of how Jesus relates to each one of us when we are in sorrow.

Mary and Martha were grief stricken at the death of their brother. No mention is made that any of them had a spouse, much less children, who could comfort them. The two sisters and their brother seemed to have only each other. So Mary and Martha were devastated when Lazarus died.

When Jesus arrived at Bethany and upon seeing Mary and Martha, he began to weep. "See how he loved him," the friends and neighbors said. Actually the people did not understand. Jesus was not crying because his good friend Lazarus was dead. He wept because Mary and Martha, whom he loved as friends, were so very distressed, and his heart went out to them. We do the same when comforting a family member or good friend on the death of someone whose love we share with them. We weep together.

We know that Jesus was not sad because he was feeling the loss of Lazarus. He had deliberately stayed away, even after learning that his friend was sick. Only upon his death did he say: "Our friend Lazarus is asleep, but I am going to awaken him." When he arrived to perform the miracle of raising the dead man (which would turn the Jewish leaders against him), he was not moved to tears until he saw the deep bereavement of the sisters and the sadness of their friends. He wept *for* and *with* them. Since he had always intended to raise Lazarus from the dead, he could not be weeping because of his own sorrow.

Yet Jesus allowed his friends to suffer as a necessary part of what he needed to accomplish, much as he wished his mother to be with him on Calvary to share his Passion. Her tear-stained face had to be painful to see. For us to recognize the eternal value of pain in the plan of redemption is to begin to comprehend divine love. In enduring any difficulty, we are never alone, for the Son of God in his life on earth fully shared sorrow and pain as part of the human condition. He knows how to weep with those he loves. To understand this and accept it gladly is so much a part of being holy.

Pain is a source of wisdom.

No saint ever had an easy life. To sacrifice one's life and one's own ambitions in order to be of service to others, in the name of Jesus, is to live according to the example of Jesus. He lived a life of humility, of service to his people in need of redemption, and eventually he suffered his Passion and death. Holiness is union with Jesus crucified in our service of others. The motivation of love is often painful.

From this perspective the life of a Christian is full of craziness to those who seek a life of power, of pleasure and of convenience. From a practical point of view, human nature avoids pain and suffering as much as possible. Actually it is unavoidable for any length of time. Some manage to find temporary diversions from the inevitability of sickness, sorrow and injustice. They might use alcohol or drugs, or find distractions in pleasurable pastimes, for which they must put the people who love them in second place.

Even a naturally good person knows that in the here and now true love is attained only when one has had to share suffering with another. The saints learn that only in welcoming those opportunities to sacrifice in union with Jesus on the cross do they grow in divine love. It is both the folly and the wisdom of suffering. There is just no other way. But to recognize the opportunities that we are given toward this end requires clear vision. Our nature tends to flee such difficulties. Often God must take that matter into his hands more directly.

To illustrate, we can compare ourselves to that stubborn animal, the mule. I have read that to get his attention it might be necessary to hit him over the head with a large piece of wood. Well, the same principle works for humans. We can be very preoccupied with personal interests and be totally unaware of the bigger picture. Something drastic is often needed to get us to focus on something more important than ourselves. We might say that God at times must get our attention by "hitting us over the head," so to speak. In the long run, it serves our situation better to accept what God sends and not make the choices of which penance to live by, since it rules out any sense of the egotistical. After all, God knows our faults better than we do and what suffering will work best. As always our example is Jesus himself.

The Romans considered scourging an accepted

form of punishment, by no means something cruel and unusual. Remember the words of Pilate to the leaders of the Jews: "I...have not found this man guilty of any of your charges against him....I will therefore have him flogged and release him" (Luke 23:14, 16). Like any criminal our Lord was tied to a post, his back was laid bare and a whip was used to lash his body unto blood. Although Jesus had committed no crime, a scourging was deemed necessary to take any fight out of him, so that he would go meekly and cause no more trouble. But there were some who would not let him go free, for he claimed to be the Son of God, a blasphemer and, as alleged by some, an enemy of Caesar.

Paul would mention that he had received thirty-nine lashes several times. Such was the punishment for one whose crime was to profess that Jesus is the Lord and Messiah. Indeed, how many martyrs throughout the centuries have suffered nearly intolerable physical pain rather than deny their friendship with Jesus?

Pain can be a friend when it warns us about a situation that could prove fatal, such as an infection, or something from without, as heat that might cause a serious burn. This we can understand. But fierce pain is nobody's friend. Yet it enters into almost every life at one time or another. Some people live with it all the time.

Sometimes it seems that the good suffer the most. We often wonder why. There is no specific answer with regard to a particular person. But if we want a general answer, we need only think about the Son of God being scourged into a bloody mess. This may not be intellectually satisfying, but at least it removes the element of self-pity.

Does God, perhaps, allow pain in our lives so he can get our attention? We often become self-centered and lose track of the truths that are eternal. When we have no uncomfortable distractions, physical discomfort does have a way of focusing us on our mortality. We will only qualify as saints when our lives reach the point that we consider suffering as something that we are privileged to share with Jesus.

The temptation of saints

Someone who has decided that sainthood is within reach may already feel that a degree of holiness has been acquired when the gross selfishness that destroys love has been eliminated from daily life. Actually it is only the beginning. The struggle now is with the temptation to spend more and more time in prayer and flee from the business of the world. This, of course, cannot be. Virtue does not consist simply in doing the right thing, but what we do must also be done for the right reason. Prayer may give us a good feeling, and that feeling may be a gift from God. But to pursue it for its own sake may stem from a false pride in one's good fortune to have been singled out by God for his special attention.

Prayer indeed keeps us in touch with God, but bringing his love to others is what unites us to the Son's work of redemption, which is true holiness. And we must be ready to go to those to whom he has chosen to send us.

We know that pride leads to all kinds of sin and is the reason we call it *capital*. In truth every sin, whatever its expression, flows from the will, which decides that something I want to do is more important than what God expects of me. Pride was the sin of Adam and Eve as well as that of Satan, who declared: "I will not serve." The sense of personal satisfaction in one's status with God is the weakness of saints that Satan can exploit. Eventually God provides ample opportunity for everyone to learn that he draws us to himself. Our holiness depends first on the power of his grace that is given to us and with which we must cooperate. The grace increases to the extent that our self-importance decreases. "He must increase, but I must decrease," said John the Baptist (John 3:30).

In what part of his sufferings might we say that Jesus atoned for these sins of pride? Was there a better way for Jesus to atone for the sins of pride of his disciples, of all future saints, than his crowning with thorns? This act began the drama of humiliations that he would endure on that fateful Friday. His other sufferings might atone for sins of sensuality but not for the sins his disciples would commit seeking spiritual power and honors.

In the not-too-distant past a man was not considered properly attired unless he wore a hat. Rules of etiquette dictated when hats must be worn, especially for women, and on what other occasions it was not appropriate to have your head covered, especially for men. Now it seems that wearing a hat, except for cold weather protection, is for police officers, military personnel and some others on formal occasions.

Maybe it is because there are not many kings and queens around anymore. But long ago it was quite the thing to cover the head with a sign of your authority or exalted position, and a royal monarch wore a gold crown, studded with jewels. Even a commoner might wear a head covering that indicated pride in his profession.

When Jesus was condemned to death because he declared himself to be the King of the Jews and therefore an enemy of Rome, it was a natural response for the soldiers to make a mockery of his claim, "...and after twisting some thorns into a crown, they put it on his head. They put a reed in his right hand and knelt before him and mocked him, saying, 'Hail, King of the Jews'" (Matthew 27:29).

A bishop who feared that he might take the honor offered him too personally once said: "Whenever I put on my miter, I try to remember the crown that Jesus wore." Saints, whatever their state in life, cultivate this same sentiment. The crown of humiliations must be worn before we wear a crown of glory. Any "official" hat should remind us that it covers the crown of our pride. As we place it on our head, we might remember the humiliated and agonizing Son of God, who allowed thorns to pierce his brow for love of us.

Carry your own cross!

We have the admonition of Jesus: "Whoever does not carry the cross and follow me cannot be my disciple" (Luke 14:27). That may be the easiest part. Before moving on, I think it necessary to think about the amount of time we spend carrying a cross that really belongs to someone else. Yet in so many ways saints are made by their willingness to take on another's cross as their own, as was Simon of Cyrene. On his journey Jesus fell several times, and the Roman soldiers wanted to make sure that he arrived alive so he could be put to death properly. They gave him help.

"As they led him away, they seized a man, Simon of Cyrene, who was coming from the country, and they laid the cross on him, and made him carry it behind Jesus" (Luke 23:26).

God did not make us self-sufficient. We began life very helpless, totally dependent on others until we grew old enough to help ourselves. Some persons are so physically or intellectually "challenged" that they depend on others for most things all their lives. But in one form or another we all are in need. This is self-evident. We readily respond to help those who are our responsibility.

The statue of the youngster carrying a younger lad on his back graces the campus of Father Flanagan's Boys' Town in Omaha, Nebraska. We might remember the story. The older boy was asked: "Is he heavy?" The inscription on the base of the statue is the answer the boy had given. "He's not heavy; he's my brother."

Those who would be holy might forget that so often we are called to carry the cross of another. How many parents have spent entire lives taking care of a disabled child? It is not so hard (not heavy) when our heart is full of love for those we are helping. The problem becomes evident to those who feel that they are getting the short end of the stick, that the situation they must endure is unjust. No one enjoys being taken advantage of.

The temptation is to say: "No more!" or like Simon, "Why me?" Yes, he had no choice, which is at times precisely our predicament. If the situation is truly unjust, of course, we may properly step away, provided nobody will be hurt, including ourselves. But that is not so easy. A protest of injustice in the workplace may bring about the loss of a job. The luxury of expressed indignation could jeopardize the well-being of one's family, and we are compelled to swallow it.

To respond with calm and even joy when we face the call to "carry someone's else's cross" is indeed heroic virtue because, when we perceive that our burden of pain is much too heavy or unfair, self-pity rears its ugly head. This may also happen when we are shouldering more than our just share of another person's responsibility. Under such conditions, without the solace of love, we feel overwhelmed.

Yes, the weight of the burden depends on the amount of love in the heart. Everyone can attest to this with varying degrees of experience. But when the extra cross we carry does not belong to someone we love and we are plagued by selfishness, there is the need to reflect on the weight that burdened those most famous shoulders, as the Son of God struggled up Calvary's hill. Simon was reluctant. We should consider it a privilege. Our quest for holiness must recognize the opportunity. The carrying of someone else's cross after Jesus, willingly, is a sure-fire way to ensure sanctity. When the situation arises to take on the burden of another's cross *a la Simon*, saints are ready to answer: "It is not so heavy. Jesus asked me to help."

The Mass reflects our oneness.

Intimacy with Jesus is the goal of sainthood, yet all the means so far considered for success on the journey will produce nothing concrete, indeed be useless, unless everything is centered in the death of Jesus that we offer in each eucharistic sacrifice with the church, the Body of Christ. During Mass we are all *reduced* to being simply *children of God,* sons and daughters of the heavenly Father. It matters not whether we are sinners or saints, young or old, men or women, educated or unlettered, priests or laity, rich or poor, healthy or sick, or certainly powerful or weak. All act with the same divine gift of faith that is not based on any human power. No one, whether pope, bishop, priest, religious or laity, can see or taste anything different. To all the Most Holy Sacrament appears the same, as bread and wine.

Success in becoming holy will depend on the degree of humility that we bring to the Mass. Jesus said that we must become as little children. This applies perhaps in no other way more than in relation to the Eucharist. We must have the simple faith of a child, as this story illustrates.

The altar server thought he was alone in the sacristy. He lifted the pall off the chalice and took the large host from the paten. Gently he kissed it. As he returned the host to its place, the priest who had entered to prepare for Mass remarked: "That was a nice gesture, Tim, but you do know that Jesus is not present until the priest calls him at the Consecration of the Mass." "Yes, Father," said Tim, "I know, but I want him to find my kiss when he comes."

We all share that boy's faith in the presence of Jesus Christ, Body and Blood, soul and divinity in the Blessed Sacrament. Yet we understand the mystery of the Eucharist no better than he in spite of great education and long life experience. For we, too, see and taste only what appears to be bread and wine. Our faith is in Jesus, Son of God, who said to his Apostles at the supper the night before he died: "'This is my body, which is given for you. Do this in remembrance of me.' And he did the same with the cup after supper, saying, 'This cup that is poured out for you is the new covenant in my blood'" (Luke 22:19–20).

By his suffering and death on the cross, Jesus redeemed us from sin. His Resurrection from the dead gave us the promise of eternal life. The sacrifice of the Mass is the memorial of that death, and when we eat his Body and drink his Blood, we receive a promise to share in his Resurrection. Thus it is truly said that the Mass is the central action of our Catholic life and the grace of the other sacraments flow from it, as with the blood that flowed from his side.

Deep reverence must underlie our prayer when we are in the presence of the eucharistic Savior. We place our commitment on the altar to be united with the sacrifice of Jesus. At the same time we want to renew our sense of awe at the divine wisdom that gave us this great Sacrament, as we view the separated "external signs." The bread (the sign of the Body of Christ) and the wine (the sign of the Blood of Christ) *signify* how Christ died, namely, his blood separated from his body. Yet he said: this *is* my body; this *is* my blood. And since Christ no longer dies, he is alive and totally present (body, blood, soul and divinity) under each sign. The Jesus we receive is the resurrected Christ as he "sits at the right hand of the Father." It is a "here and now" experience of Jesus, not just a re-enactment of history.

Then the receiving of Holy Communion is in response to Jesus who said: "Take and eat; this is my body, which was given for you. Take and drink: this is my blood, which was shed for you." Thus we expect to experience the strength that comes from such intimacy, and we are determined to serve him with the joy of love.

Son and mother together again

The sacrifice of the Mass is where we encounter Jesus most personally, and here, too, we must not separate the son from the mother. As Mary was present beside the cross on Calvary, she is present whenever her Son's sacrifice is renewed. Again we unite with Jesus through Mary to become one with our Redeemer. We benefit from the holy sacrifice if we place ourselves alongside Mary so that our Mass will truly become the moment when we are closest to Jesus.

Think about this. If a priest were celebrating a Mass of Thanksgiving on the twenty-fifth anniversary of his ordination, who would be sitting "front and center"? The place would be reserved for the priest's mother (and father), even if some very distinguished people were also present. After all, who in the congregation could possibly outrank the mother of the priest who is celebrating the Mass?

The priest's mother should have the first place for a greater reason than human courtesy. Was not Mary standing beside the cross on Calvary? Since the human priest at the altar acts "in the person of Jesus," the woman closest to the front should represent the mother of Jesus, and who better than the mother of the celebrating priest?

A saint attends Mass as often as possible, even daily, but the Sunday liturgy is especially efficacious for our sense of unity with Jesus, because we are together as the church, the Body of Christ. Sanctity is not for loners. Mary is present even when the priest does not celebrate with any notable sense of dignity, or preaches badly, or the congregational singing leaves much to be desired. Circumstances which make the Mass more emotionally inspiring, spiritually fulfilling or even enjoyable should be hoped for, since these can generate a greater sense of community as the people of God. We come together because Jesus expects his people to gather as his Body the church. He wants us to celebrate our faith in his Resurrection, to share in his death on the cross as our strength and salvation, and be together with our brothers and sisters who possess with us the life of God through baptism.

We might say that Mary, the mother of Jesus, invites us to join her at Mass because she was with her Son on Good Friday. We know that her presence on Calvary was no accident. Jesus wanted her there. He could have made sure that she was safe at home in Nazareth, protected from witnessing the horrible events of that day. But he knew that she must be with him. By the will of the Father, she had to offer him and to suffer with him, in order that she might give birth to the church and thus become our mother also. At Mass, as mother of the church, she offers him again with us.

CHAPTER EIGHT

better days ahead

I consider that the sufferings of this present
time are not worth comparing with the glory
about to be revealed to us.
—Romans 8:18

The process of becoming holy is rightfully seen
as being drawn steadily into a love relationship with
the Triune God, the Father, the Son and the Holy
Spirit, which began at our baptism, the moment of our
birth with God's life. Jesus, the Son who became man,
is our connection to the Father and the Holy Spirit.
Hence, the more intimate our relationship to Jesus,
the holier we are said to be. He told the Apostles:
"Believe me that I am in the Father and the Father is
in me.... On that day you will know that I am in my
Father, and you in me, and I in you.... But the
Advocate, the Holy Spirit, whom the Father will send
in my name, will teach you everything, and remind
you of all that I have said to you" (John 14:11, 20, 26).

By nature some relationships are forever while
others are temporary. Friends, for instance, come and

go, because there is no intrinsic connection. They were made by choice. Rare is the one who is still close to a friend from childhood years, or even from adolescence. Yet there are some relationships that never end.

Our father and mother, for example, will be our parents even after their deaths. Death ends their relationship as husband and wife. They will be "related," however, for eternity because of the child (or children) their love brought into being. Also our brothers and sisters (and other blood relatives) can never be shaken loose, because we are connected to them through our parents. It does not matter that we never knew them, or that we have not seen them for a very long time.

Yet all these relationships did not always exist, but began at some simultaneous moment in time. Only one relationship can be called eternal in the strict sense, that is, without beginning or end. That, of course, is the relationship in God between the Father and the Son and the Holy Spirit, which we speak of as the Most Holy Trinity. This is the fundamental mystery of faith, because it pertains to the very life of God. His nature is love, and we are created according to his image. We have been called to this relationship, and we therefore say that to be holy is to be in love with God. Yet love is free and is only possible to creatures of intelligence and will.

Let us review our basic learning experience in catechism class when we asked: "Who is God?" The singular verb is correct because there is only *one* God. Yet, I have often wondered whether we might properly also ask: "Who *are* God?" since the pronoun *who* is used when we are looking for a name. The term God signifies *nature* and Father, Son and Holy Spirit signify *persons.* So three persons are *one* God. Jesus proved that he was indeed the Son of God as he said, and he told us about his Father and the Holy Spirit. And we *believe* him.

With theological accuracy we can say that God *are* three divine persons in *one* divine nature. Yet we also say, more personally, "God is Love." This phrase does not simply mean that he loves us, or that he is the source of all love. Rather, his very *nature* is love, because of the eternal relationships that exist between these three distinct persons, who are united in one being and are therefore inseparable.

We have all been baptized in the name of the Father and of the Son and of the Holy Spirit. As children of God we are, in an analogous sense, the "fruit" of their love. Hence we are all "related" with an eternal relationship that will never end and is more important to us than any human relationship. That is why Jesus expects us to love one another as he has loved us.

Spiritual relationships are eternal.

Through our spirit we have relationships that will never end. As children of God still on earth, we are related to those who have already gone to heaven and also to those who wait in purgatory until their entrance into glory. These latter are sometimes called "the Poor Souls," and I do not know why. The souls in hell are the pitiful ones, always remembering *what could have been.* In the language of time those "waiting" in purgatory are actually full of joyous anticipation, since they are aware of their eventual entry into heaven. But again we are speaking in temporal terms. Eternity has a language all its own. We who are still "in time" are still being formed in that eternal relationship.

With regard to the souls in purgatory I prefer the proper form, which is, "the faithful departed." We understand that some might need a period of purgation to be totally purified, so as to be worthy of the eternal joys of the heavenly kingdom. Thus we pray for those who have lived in union with Jesus on earth when we say: "May these and all the faithful departed through the mercy of God rest in peace." We firmly believe in the justice of God and his mercy, upon which we all rely at the moment of death.

The church joins the celebration of the Feast of All Saints on November 1, that is, those already enjoying the beatific vision, with All Souls Day on November 2, making this the month of the faithful departed. We are encouraged to pray for our beloved dead at this time. Joining as the communion of saints with those who have gone before us, some in glory and some awaiting glory, we are made to realize that the day will come when we will join them.

Since no one can be sure when that day will be, we ought to think seriously about the day when our own journey will end, the day of our death. Does that thought bring a smile to our faces, or fear in our hearts? The degree of our joy and anticipation measures the level of holiness we have attained. Saints live joyfully in anticipation of meeting Jesus face to face.

Would you consider it a blessing to be called to God suddenly, without any warning, such as, in one's sleep, or following a fatal stroke or heart attack? The most frequent comment that we hear when someone dies in this way is: "What a wonderful way to go."

But I really wonder if it is such a blessing to die unexpectedly. It seems to me that such a departure "cheats" one from a chance to *enjoy a happy death* with family and friends. Why not celebrate our victory over sin and death with them for a few weeks or a month? Over the years I have been edified and strengthened by witnessing the joy manifested by so many that I have assisted at their death. One woman I remember was so happy that I could not help expressing the wish that I was going with her.

Our faith-filled joy as we look forward to an eternity of blessedness in the kingdom of heaven (with Jesus, Mary and all our departed loved ones) would be a grace that our family and friends would never forget. I know that, as long as my mind is clear, I am hoping for at least a month. Why fear death when Jesus is waiting for us?

Eyes on the horizon

Each culture has different ways to remember the events of national, family or personal importance. The manner of remembering is not so important as the need to do so, because human beings tend to focus directly on what is happening in the present moment and forget who and what got us to where we are now.

The church, in her wisdom, knows this. So each year, more than any other time, she celebrates the most important event in the history of the world with special exuberance, namely, the Resurrection of Jesus from the dead. We have a period of penance for forty days when we share the cross of Jesus, and this we conclude with the commemoration of his Passion on Good Friday. We need to be constantly reminded that through Christ's sufferings and death the human race was restored to grace. Only by dying with him do we become eligible for an eternal life of glory. Remembering always that Jesus has shown us that by rising from the dead he has power over death, the saints retained confidence in the promise to his faithful followers that we, too, will arise to eternal glory in the kingdom of heaven.

Yes, we are an *alleluia* people, believing in Jesus Risen. Everything else we believe and do rests on that truth. As Saint Paul says, "If Christ has not been raised, your faith is futile and you are still in your sins" (1 Corinthians 15:17). We need to remember this in every circumstance of our lives, in the difficult times but also in the good times. We cannot afford to be soothed into a sense of complacency. Joy is the most evident expression of our faith, and this faith is the source of all peace. When our spirit of joy is constant, we will have reached the goal of sanctity and every moment will be one of peace. But like love, peace is not something we pursue head-on. One day it just surprises us.

Of course, to attain this end our constant companion must be the Lord's mother, Mary, who did not forget his promise to rise from the dead. Unlike the Apostles and Mary Magdalene, she was not surprised when he appeared at her doorstep that first day of the week. She was happy. She was expecting him, and her hours of loneliness were over.

Yet Mary also knew that her time with him would be short, that in forty days he would return to his

Father and send the Holy Spirit. Her Son would be beyond her sight, too. She would remain to live her life of faith, together with the Apostles and the early church. From this point on, the day of Pentecost, we all begin our journey toward holiness. At this moment, since we have not been called to the Father, we live the time of Pentecost within the life of the church. Through the power of the Spirit who permeates our lives, we respond to the call of holiness. Even so, this vocation to sanctity remains a challenge because of the selfishness that plagues our sinful nature.

How long will that take? Would that it was as short and easy as the answer a child gave in catechism class to the question: "How long does it take to get to heaven?" His reply was: "Five days." His reasoning could not be simpler. Jesus promised to send the Holy Spirit when he returned to heaven. He left on Ascension Thursday. Ten days later the Holy Spirit arrived. So it took each of them five days.

And how long will it take you to get to heaven? It will certainly take more than five days. Indeed, we know it takes a lifetime, but we are confident that the Holy Spirit will give us the perseverance it takes.

Until the day of Pentecost, the Apostles were a cowardly lot, very fearful. They had a right to be, for they did not quite understand what was expected of them, other than "to go and teach all nations." For such a band of simple and basically inexperienced men, what a command! They were hiding in the upper room "for fear of the Jews." But then came the "tongues of fire" and the "rushing wind." Suddenly, they were bold. No longer did fear grip them. No longer were they uncertain.

The obvious difference in their behavior resulted from the power of the Holy Spirit, as promised by Jesus. They obtained new *gifts*, which gave them knowledge (power to believe what Jesus had taught); understanding (power to trust that Jesus would keep his promises to them); and wisdom (power to be loyal to Jesus out of love). These were received together with the total awareness of God's goodness toward all his people (counsel), with a sense of awe that God would work much good through them (piety) and with a certitude that their strength came from God and would always be with them (fortitude). They would no longer rely on their own strength. This allowed no room for fear (except of the Lord).

The sense of fear can surround us for many reasons, namely, physical danger, our declining health, financial insecurity, fear of ridicule, a fear of failures and many more. Sadly, most of the time we worry about them before they happen.

How tragic, and what a waste of time and energy! Often nothing does go wrong. That is often more good luck than good management on our part. And the "good luck" is God watching over us. The biggest tragedy of all would be not to try anything new because it would cause some inconvenience, or pain, or might even prove unsuccessful.

There are no timid saints. They are generally aware in each waking moment that the Holy Spirit is present in the church and within each of us. Those aspiring to holiness make every effort to flee the shadows of doubt that can creep over us when we review past failures or insecurities. What is done is done; what is ahead is the possible. With the Spirit of God impelling us, we will find that sanctity and boldness become inseparable.

To forget is possible.

Lest we become overconfident, however, we need to take time to review the situation with the Apostles, who heard from Jesus himself the prediction of his Passion and his Resurrection. "From that time on, Jesus began to show his disciples that he must go to Jerusalem and undergo great suffering at the hands of the elders and chief priests and scribes, and be killed and on the third day be raised" (Matthew 16:21).

The Gospels indicate that Jesus instructed his Apostles many times about his impending death and subsequent Resurrection from the dead after three days. After they experienced a glimpse of his glory at the Transfiguration, Jesus commanded them: "Tell no one about the vision until after the Son of Man has been raised from the dead" (Matthew 17:9).

Yet on the third morning, the day after the Sabbath, we find Mary Magdalene on her way to the tomb. She and the other women "bought spices, so that they might go and anoint him" (Mark 16:1). Having seen the empty tomb, Mary, who did not recognize Jesus and took him for the gardener, beseeched him: "Sir, if you have carried him away, tell me where you have laid him, and I will take him away" (John 20:15). In her sadness, she could not remember "the promise."

After she realized the truth, Mary and the others went to tell the Apostles: "...and returning from the tomb, they told all this to the eleven and to all the rest....But these words seemed to them an idle tale, and they did not believe them" (Luke 24:9, 11). Even with the evidence of eyewitnesses, the Apostles forgot the promise of Jesus that he would be raised from the dead. How could they now still refuse to believe? That evening, even after the rest had seen Jesus and told Thomas: "We have seen the Lord," he would declare, "Unless I...put...my hand in his side, I will not believe" (John 20:25).

Yet it had been all laid out for them beforehand. It was after eliciting from Peter the declaration: "You are the Messiah, the Son of the Living God" (Matthew 16:16), that Jesus told them what would happen in Jerusalem, about his impending Passion, death and his Resurrection after three days. Strangely, it seems that they never really wanted to understand him. They would not imagine that a resurrection would be necessary, because they could not make themselves think about his suffering and death that would have to come first. No wonder that, when it all came about, the crucifixion surprised them, fear entered in and they were in no position to remember the glorious conclusion. Yes, they forgot the most important part.

Even saints should not be alarmed at the Apostles' forgetfulness. Can we not all remember times when we forgot "the promise" of Resurrection when Good Friday was upon us? Since it is discomforting to take up the cross that is suddenly thrust upon us, at that crucial moment we tend to forget "the promise." Yet saints ought never be surprised.

Are we not in all things to be "as little children"? Most well-balanced youngsters are eternal optimists. They sometimes even hope against hope, believing every pledge given, no matter by whom or how outlandish and self-serving on the part of the one who offers so much. Not with the naïveté of children who often forget the conditions that attach to a promise, but with their sense of confidence, those who would be holy trust in the promise of the one whose Passion they share.

Adults who never trust anyone under any circumstances or else trust everyone without question might be deemed socially dysfunctional. Eventually, experience should bring balance, but actions that are based on such false hopes may have already led to a long string of painful experience. Can we ask which is worse: the too trusting or the too skeptical, to act on a promise that was not sincere; or to act on a promise that was misunderstood?

For any Christian to live on promises not made by God is the sin of *superstition*. One horrendous example is the practice of chain letters, which promise infallible results when certain prayers are said for nine days, nine copies left in a church or mailed to friends, and a promise to give thanks for the favor received by publication in a newspaper or magazine. This is a case of hollow faith, of spiritual gullibility.

Yet many decisions in our daily life are based on promises made by another. On the top of the list, of course, is the "I do" of the marriage ceremony. Every contract we sign is a promise to fulfill the conditions. That includes employment contracts, rent contracts, insurance contracts and so on, as well as such simple promises as: "I will pick you up at seven o'clock in front of the post office," or "Your car will be ready by ten o'clock." We rely on weather reports each morning to guide us in our vesture before we leave the house.

To live by promises, therefore, belongs to the natural rhythm of life. In order to reach the ultimate goal of heaven, it is reasonable to look to the information we have from divine faith coupled with the promises so clearly proclaimed in the Scriptures.

The divine promise came from the mouth of Jesus himself: "I am the resurrection and the life. Those who believe in me, even though they die, will live, and everyone who lives and believes in me will never die" (John 11:25–26). But saints do not forget the condition: "If any want to become my followers, let them deny themselves and take up their cross daily and follow me" (Luke 9:23). Holiness demands absolute trust in the word of the one who first rose from the dead, a prediction he made well before he died. The heart sings "alleluia" and assures the saint that disappointment is not something to be feared.

Saints are never lonely.

The gift of prayer that is given by the Holy Spirit to all who truly seek God may seem to draw one into oneself and discourage a relationship with people. But that would not be holiness. Prayer is not meant to make one feel so close to Jesus that to withdraw from human contacts as much as possible is something to be desired. That would not bring one closer to God, but rather closer to one's own selfish being. Prayer indeed focuses us on the essence of holiness, union with the Triune God. We become holy, however, only through the relationship of charity we develop with others precisely because we have a relationship to the Father through Jesus in the Holy Spirit. After all, are not all the baptized related to the Triune God and therefore adopted children of God, as I am? We cannot separate ourselves from them and expect to attain holiness.

We may truly believe that all three persons of the Blessed Trinity are distinct and equal and are the one God who created us, who redeemed us and who now brings us to holiness. We are sincere when we pray "In the name of the Father and of the Son and of the Holy Spirit," in whom we were baptized. Too often, however, in our private prayer, we separate them one from the other. We pray to the Father with no reference to the Son, or to Jesus as if he stands alone, or to the Holy Spirit when we are concerned about wisdom, or strength, or courage, or understanding.

The Father loved us and sent the Son to redeem us. Jesus obeyed the will of his Father in order to glorify him by offering himself on the cross for us. He is our example and the one whom we are called to imitate, to follow as his disciples, in order to attain salvation. But to do this we need the fire of the Holy Spirit.

We see that Jesus alone did not accomplish it for the Apostles. Three years of his presence, listening to his teaching from his own lips, watching his miracles and being captivated by that dynamic personality did not prevent them from turning into cowards at the moment of testing. Almost to the end they fought over who would be the greatest in the kingdom. They misunderstood their mission even on the way to the mount of the Ascension.

But when the Holy Spirit came down on them at Pentecost, they became fearless, finally understanding what Jesus had been saying all along. In his promise to send the Holy Spirit, he had said: "But the

Advocate, the Holy Spirit, whom the Father will send in my name, will teach you everything, and remind you of all that I have said to you" (John 14:26).

The church, in her most public and perfect prayer, the Mass, does not separate the three persons in God. We must listen attentively and notice how often the three persons are all mentioned together and in their proper relationship, namely, the Father who sent the Son and the Spirit whom the Son sent from the Father on Pentecost.

For example, note the opening lines of Eucharistic Prayer III: "Father, you are holy indeed and all creation rightly gives you praise. All life, all holiness comes from you through your Son, Jesus Christ our Lord, by the working of the Holy Spirit."

In prayer we must recognize that the three persons are all in it together.

This may be easy to experience when our relationship with those who share with us the life of grace is running smoothly. But know that much of the time it does not, because we are all in the struggling mode as human beings. Even those who love us have a way of making our lives difficult, as we do theirs. We are inclined to remove any degree of fault from ourselves, see the culpability in everyone else and, in fact, think that God has let us down. Saints learn to look to themselves for the fault.

To attain holiness we need to acknowledge our own inadequacies and accept responsibility for whatever has gone wrong in our lives. If we still want to place the fault with someone else, or on a circumstance that was beyond our control, then we are far from sainthood.

For some strange reason we might even blame one whom we know loves us the most, if we decide that a promise has been forgotten or even broken. We might, in fact, be lamenting: "I am so angry (*read*: disappointed) in God." That in itself is not so terrible, since even the prophets of the Old Testament frequently got annoyed with God's ways, and the great Teresa of Avila sometimes complained to Jesus that he might be a little more cooperative in her efforts to do the work he had commissioned of her. When we are inclined, however, to direct some anger or disappointment or annoyance toward the Almighty, let us be sure we direct our *mad* at the right person. After all, only someone with free will, a *person*, can be blamed for harming you, but God is (are) *three* persons, and we must choose which one we feel has betrayed us.

So, then, shall we blame the Father, who created us to inherit the kingdom of heaven? Could he not make everything work out to our advantage, if he wanted to? But we remember that when man renounced the divine inheritance through sin, the Father did not abandon us but even sent his Son to satisfy for our sinfulness by his death on the cross, which returned us to his grace. So then ought we get mad at the Holy Spirit? That would mean that the wisdom, justice, peace and understanding, or the strength, prudence and a spirit of wonder which he gives are not sufficient to raise us above our difficulties here and show us their value for eternal life.

So, then, that leaves us with the Son. Yet since he came to share our human miseries, not to take them away, it becomes hard to single out the second person for criticism. We might foolishly end up blaming all three, the Father, the Son and the Holy Spirit. Since the Incarnate Son understands our difficulties better, being one of us, he ought to receive the brunt of our annoyance.

Be warned, however, that if we wish to complain to the Son, we must do so on our knees before his tortured figure hanging upon the cross and have our say as we gaze into his face. That always returns a saint to the wisdom that has been temporarily forgotten.

The deficiencies of human judgment

In reviewing the long list of saints who have been placed before us by the church as examples of the highest Christian charity, I find it especially interesting that they run the gamut from kings to simple peasants, popes to parish priests, renowned theologians to unknown religious and a myriad of other contrasts that would take books to speak about. All of this only shows that the essence of sanctity is the grace given by the Holy Spirit to those who fulfill God's holy will in whatever garden the flower has been planted. We must keep all of this in mind as we respond to each challenge that people and events present to us along the journey toward the perfection of charity.

People who lack the emotional and spiritual depth of true holiness often seek solutions to interrelational problems, even within the church, in human understanding and experience. But let us look to Jesus. From the perspective of organizational acumen and public relations savvy, Jesus could not have picked a more unlikely group to be his Apostles and the first bishops of his church. An honest appraisal of their qualifications would hardly prompt any of us to give them the responsibility of leading, teaching and guiding an enterprise that was intended "to reach to the ends of the earth."

Most of these men were accustomed to hard physical labor as fishermen, uneducated and with no social standing. Matthew had a profession (a despised tax collector), and Judas was possibly some kind of an accountant since he managed the common purse (*cf.* John 13:29). Did you ever wonder why Jesus, if he were looking for good will among the people and their leaders, did not tap Joseph of Arimathea or Nicodemus? They were respected by all, and later on did prove themselves faithful. The Lord seems to have gone out of his way to pick those least likely to succeed.

Two deficiencies stand out that did not recommend the Apostles for true spiritual leadership, namely, their cowardice and their unabashed ambition for glory. In the hour of crisis, they fled for their lives from the garden of Gethsemane and then hid in the upper room "for fear of the Jews." Peter, their leader, who returned secretly to follow Jesus into the courtyard of the High Priest, lost courage when he was discovered. Only John, the youngest, was around for the crucifixion.

We can surmise that their expectations had been crushed. One time Jesus heard them discussing which of them would be the greatest in the new kingdom, and he reprimanded them: "Whoever wants to be first must be last of all and servant of all" (Mark 9:35). We know that they had expected something better for the time that had been invested in Jesus, for even on the way to the mount of the Ascension they were still concerned about an earthly kingdom (*cf.* Acts 1:6).

After Jesus ascended to his Father, the Apostles awaited the promised coming of the Holy Spirit who would help them understand all that Jesus had taught. They remembered his words: "Go, therefore and make disciples of all nations, baptizing them in the name of the Father and of the Son and of the Holy Spirit" (Matthew 28:19). But how are we to do this? Who will help us? How long will it take? The Romans will kill us first.

But when the Holy Spirit descended on them with the fire of love and the strong wind of courage, they were transformed into men of strength and self-confidence, without fear and with uncompromising trust in the promises of Jesus. The Savior had indeed chosen the weak and made them strong.

Saints eventually learn to rely on the judgment of Jesus, strengthened in the assurance that the Lord has reasons for choosing whom he does. The deficiencies that human judgment might find in someone who has been called to be a disciple gives way to a sense of gratitude for one's own good fortune in being chosen. Jesus knows more than we do what is ahead and whom he needs. That is a comforting thought.

This awareness is very helpful when, although with spiritual motives, we find ourselves interiorly disturbed by what is happening around us. We realize that our expectations are not totally prompted by the spirit but by our own interests and that we still have a way to go on our road to holiness.

The continuing guidance of Mary
Certainly all of us fortunate enough to have had loving and strict parents can always rely on the memory

of our mother's admonitions, especially during adolescence, to keep us checking in when we venture into dangerous waters. We want to please her, to have her proud of us, even into our mature years, probably more than when we were young. For some of us this applies to our fathers as well.

So do we have a mother whom we want to please in matters that concern the spirit? We certainly do. She is the mother of Jesus whom he shared with us from the cross: "Behold thy mother!" So it goes without saying that no one comes close to Jesus except through Mary. No one becomes a saint unless guided and protected by the Queen of Saints herself. There must be consciously present in each one who yearns to be holy a desire to please her, who is closer to Jesus than any other creature. She who is the daughter of the Father, the mother of the Son and the spouse of the Holy Spirit is the indispensable link with the life of the Triune God. Every saint has a deep love of Mary and an abiding devotion to her as our mother. The proper expression of this devotion, for our personal growth, is the recitation of her rosary in which she accompanies us through the moments that make up the mystery of our redemption. She comforts and rejoices with us as we travel through the joyful, sorrowful and glorious mysteries of our own lives. She guides us through the mysteries of light as mother of the church.

When we think of our Blessed Mother, are we comfortable with the thought that she is also our queen? To love Mary as mother with all its emotional bonding and to honor her as the queen of heaven may create a certain ambivalent feeling. Is it similar to the idea of

Jesus as both our brother *and* our king? She is truly our mother and our queen.

I am reminded of the young boy who for the first time saw his mother dressed in a formal gown. He stood wide-eyed and exclaimed: "Mommy, you are so beautiful!" The next morning, seeing her in the kitchen as she prepared breakfast, he gave her a hug and declared: "I like you better this way. Now you look like a mother."

If we find it hard to grasp that Mary and Jesus are united as king and queen, as well as mother and son, we might be tempted to think of Mary simply as the Queen Mother, that is, the mother of the king. However, that would be shortsighted. We believe that she is truly the queen of heaven and earth, and thus she shares in his dignity and power. Christ by nature deserves the title of king, and he chose his mother to rule with him, as she first suffered with him on Calvary. "He is the image of the invisible God, the firstborn of all creation; for in him all things in heaven and on earth were created, things visible and invisible, whether thrones or dominions or rulers or powers—all things have been created through him and for him" (Colossians 1:15–16).

Does this not say that Christ is king of creation by the Father's will from the beginning? We can properly ask if he was also to have a queen from the beginning, who would share his glory and power. Of course, we know that with the "change in perspective" by the sin of Adam, the Son of God had first to redeem his kingdom from sin. This meant that he had to come, not as a king in glory, but as a savior. Our king, then, came among us as a helpless infant with his glory hidden.

BETTER DAYS AHEAD

He was born as a brother to us, subject like us to every human frailty except sin. His second coming will be one of glory.

And what about his queen? She too awaits that final glory, and until then she serves him as a virginal mother and participates in his redemptive mission. She gave our king to us as a brother, and he gave his queen to us as a mother. We are blessed with a brother and a mother to lead us to salvation and then bring us to eternal glory.

So in our pursuit of holiness we will be successful only if we keep everything in perspective. Reciting the rosary with Mary, we remember how the Son of God, our king, was born in the stable at Bethlehem, an unlikely palace. He became brother to us. His queen became his mother and mother to us all. King and queen sound nice, but mother and brother have a more comfortable feel for us poor sinners. Yet we need to remember also that our king ruled first from the throne of the cross with a crown of thorns on his head. We should not expect to enjoy here on earth any greater dignity, for as his disciples we must become one with him and wait to join him and our mother in the glory of heaven.

Home is where the heart is.

Immigrants have to be a hearty lot. Leaving familiar surroundings and relocating somewhere new is a deeply emotional experience, more so when the move is to a far away place. The adventurous find it exhilarating. The fearful always anticipate many difficulties. In some instances the people left behind suffer more anxiety than those setting out to begin a new life. Also, although the move is to a different country or area, it frequently happens that the heart goes nowhere, but remains at the old homestead.

I often wonder if Jesus, from a human perspective, was a bit excited about returning home, even though he was leaving the fear-filled Apostles and, of course, his mother. Jesus knew that they would follow him to be with the Father. As he had reminded them: "I am the way, and the truth, and the life. No one comes to the Father except through me" (John 14:6).

Forty days after his Resurrection Jesus ascends to his Father. Before he leaves, he promises the Apostles: "I go to prepare a place for you" (John 14:2). He has trained them for the leadership of his church and must leave so that the Holy Spirit can come to them with fire and energy, enlightenment and strength. "If I do not go away, the Advocate will not come to you; but if I go, I will send him to you" (John 16:7).

Although only Jesus truly "came from heaven" (*cf.* John 3:13), we know that, as the adopted children of God, we have inherited heaven as our true home. This world is a temporary stay, where we grow in holiness so as to be ever more worthy of this gift. The expectation of an eternity united intimately with the Father, Son and Holy Spirit takes on a special delight in the thought that Mary, Joseph and our loved ones are part of the package deal. Yet, we so often feel reluctant to leave this home. Is it because our heart is not really in our true home? We may only be afraid of moving to a new and basically unknown place.

Attachment to the things of this world, or to the people who share our world with us, makes it difficult to think about leaving our earthly abode. Also it is sometimes better not to think too much about "our journey home," or else we might just sit back and wait. God expects us to make good use of whatever time we have remaining, and he will let us know when he is ready. With the strength of his grace, we will get excited about our "going home," when the time is imminent.

Meanwhile, we wait for the hour of departure to arrive, half in joyful anticipation and half in a timid hope that it will not be too soon. We might pray for the outlook of the saints, who longed to leave this world. Their prayer each day often began with the lament: "O Lord, how much longer?"